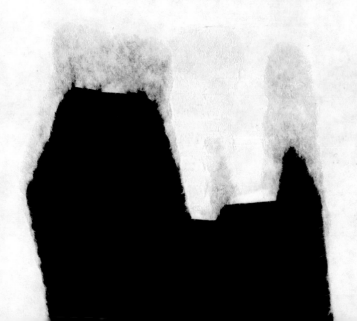

Portuguese colonialism in Africa:
the end of an era

Portuguese colonialism in Africa: *the end of an era*

The effects of Portuguese colonialism on education, science, culture and information

by Eduardo de Sousa Ferreira
with an introduction
by Basil Davidson

The Unesco Press
Paris 1974

Published by
The Unesco Press
Place de Fontenoy, 75700 Paris
Printed by Maison d'Edition, Marcinelle

ISBN 92-3-101163-4
French edition 92-3-201163-8

Preface

The 1960s saw most of the formerly colonial peoples achieve their independence. Some colonial territories however remain. Until recently the most striking were those in white-controlled South Africa and included the Portuguese colonies.

The situation has now changed dramatically. The former Prime Minister, Marcello Caetano, was toppled by a *coup d'état* in Portugal led by officers of the Portuguese army themselves opposed to colonial wars Portugal could not win, by the growing feeling the wars strained Portugal's resources, and by a desire to start a new era both within Portugal and with the African countries she had once colonized.

This work, *Portuguese Colonialism in Africa: the End of an Era; the Effects of Portuguese Colonialism,* is an attempt to analyse former Portuguese policy in key areas of Unesco's concern. It should be seen within the framework of the United Nations—and Unesco's—commitment to decolonization. It is also an attempt to measure Portuguese policy and practice against international norms. In some ways, it is a companion volume to *Apartheid. Its Effects on Education, Science, Culture and Information,* first published by Unesco in 1967.

This book was written before the new government took power. The material was collected up to November 1973. Since that time, the new Portuguese Government has publicly recognized the right of its colonies to independence and to self-determination. It has recognized the independence of Guinea-Bissau and has supported that country's application for admission to the United Nations and other international organizations, including Unesco; in Mozambique it has appointed an interim government which includes members of the

Mozambique Liberation Front (FRELIMO); and in Angola it has set in motion the process of decolonization.

The former Government of Portugal withdrew from Unesco on 31 December 1972. On 12 September 1974 Portugal rejoined the Organization. In a policy speech at the eighteenth session of the General Conference on 21 October 1974, the Minister of Education and Culture, Professor Magalhaes Godinho, summed up the goals of the new government in choosing the path of total decolonization:

> It is not just a question of a major contribution to world peace, it is also—need I say, above all?—a question of a new attitude towards man and towards men; we intend to respect personal and cultural individuality, to give every person the chance to build his life in accordance with his own plan and every society the opportunity to follow its own freely-chosen paths to development. The end of the colonialist policy, which was in any case unpopular with most of the Portuguese people, means recognition of the overriding value of human rights for men as individuals and as living societies and cultures; it has also, in Portugal itself, sounded the death knell of political, economic and cultural oppression.

The relevance of this book is now threefold. It puts in historical perspective today's events; it gives information on the situation from which the new States will start; finally it is an analysis of the functioning of major social institutions in a colonial country.

In the preparation of this report, the Secretariat requested relevant information from the Government of Portugal as well as permission for a member of the Secretariat to be allowed to collect information within the territories. The then Government of Portugal refused these requests.

The sources for the present study are: (a) primary sources where these are available; it was found however that much Portuguese material, when it was available, was outdated, unreliable and provided little basis for cross-country comparisons; (b) secondary sources: newspapers, interviews, etc. In this connexion, the Secretariat wishes to thank in particular the United Nations Library; Patricia Tsien of the United Nations staff; the Swedish Institute for Development and Aid, Stockholm; the Scandinavian Institute of African Studies, Uppsala, the White Fathers, Rome; the Library of Congress, Washington; the African Studies Center, Los Angeles, California; the Arnold Bergsträsser Institut, Freiburg, as well as Ulric Cross, Dean, Faculty of Law, University of Dar-es-Salaam, and I. Yastrebova, Senior Research Worker of the Africa Institute of the U.S.S.R. Academy of Sciences, Moscow. We also wish to thank Karin de Sousa Ferreira for her assistance in translation and Frank McDermott for his careful editing of the final manuscript.

The report was established for Unesco by Eduardo de Sousa Ferreira. The introduction is by Basil Davidson.

The views expressed in the report are those of the authors and are not necessarily those of the Secretariat.

October 1974

Contents

Portuguese colonial values

An introduction by Basil Davidson

The blacks in Africa must be directed and organized by Europeans but are indispensable as auxiliaries . . . [and] must be regarded as productive elements organised or to be organised in an economy directed by the whites.

Marcello Caetano, former Portuguese Prime Minister[1]

We alone, before anyone else, brought to Africa the notion of human rights and racial equality. We alone practiced the principle of multi-racialism, which all now consider to be the most perfect and daring expression of human brotherhood and sociological progress. . . . Our African provinces are more developed, more progressive in every respect than any recently independent territory in Africa south of the Sahara, without exception.

Franco Nogueira, former Portuguese Foreign Minister[2]

While the bulk of this study was made before the dramatic events of 1974 and the overthrow of the Portuguese dictatorship, its value today is pershaps still larger than before. To the extent of Portuguese decolonization, what are the problems which the emergent nations of Angola, Guinea-Bissau and Mozambique must now confront and try to solve? In the cultural and scientific fields, as in other fields, what are their factual 'starting points'? Upon what ground do they now stand: with what handicaps, with what advantages drawn from their long and difficult national struggle? Dr Ferreira's study is an important contribution towards answering these hard but necessary questions.

1. Written while Marcello Caetano (overthrown in April 1974) was teaching as a professor of the University of Coimbra: *Os Nativos na Economia Africana*, p. 16, 1954.
2. In his book, *The Third World*, p. 154–5, 1967, written while Dr Nogueira was Foreign Minister.

Those who have studied the affairs of Portugal, whether there or in Africa, have disagreed in many of their judgements, for the whole subject has long become remote and controversial. But on two points they have generally reached a full agreement. They have found a warm affection and respect for the Portuguese people; and these are sentiments which speak from almost every serious study of the subject, however variously expressed and with whatever reservations. The second point of general agreement turns on a rather different matter. It consists in an always present and often acute difficulty in obtaining reliable information, above all detailed information, on the way that the Portuguese really live, and on the way that others under their control must live.

This difficulty has a variety of origins. But generally it has arisen from a deficiency of established or admitted information, notably statistical, linked to the use of an official idiom of explanation often bafflingly contradictory or ambiguous. There have been times when the spokesmen of official Portugal, of a régime in power for nearly half a century, have seemed perfectly unaware of the contrary implications that others may or must logically draw from what they claim or aver. Or there have been times when such spokesmen or exegisists, including the most powerful men in the land, have appeared to be living in a world of fantasy that others cannot recognize as real. No doubt all countries have displayed examples of this kind. None seem so persistent or extraordinary as those provided by the rulers of the Portuguese.

The sentences quoted at the beginning of this chapter are fair specimens. Of these, the first appears as a concise realistic statement about the truths of colonial doctrine; there is no difficulty in understanding it, and no possibility of drawing implications other than those intended by the writer. The since deposed head of the Portuguese Government, after Salazar, considers that Africans can be useful in so far as they are controlled and organized by the whites, not as individuals here and there but as whole peoples, as a kind of humanity to be regarded as inherently and naturally inferior to white humanity. That former Prime Minister Caetano regarded Africans in this way is clear, moreover, not only from the further context of his doctrinal utterances but also from many subsequent statements and explanations.

Now this is a familiar point of view, although one that its adherents, nowadays, may seldom care to defend as openly as this. But how is this point of view to be put together with the views of one of Professor

Caetano's most respected political colleagues, Dr Franco Nogueira? Like Prime Minister Caetano, Dr Nogueira was for long a foremost exponent of Portuguese policy and a close associate of Dr Caetano's. On the great issues of the world today, these two men see undoubtedly the same picture, and find in it the same answers. Yet here is Dr Nogueira, when Foreign Minister, telling us that Portugal's systematic subordination of the Africans of its overseas territories as 'auxiliaries', as 'productive elements organised or to be organised in an economy directed by the whites', is none the less equivalent to 'the most perfect and daring expression of human brotherhood and sociological progress'. And in case we may think that he must be surely talking of some altogether different subject he goes on to affirm, quite without the shadow of a doubt or hesitation, that Portugal's territories in Africa are more developed and progressive 'than any recently independent territory in Africa south of the Sahara, without exception'. Even the soberest of researchers, when confronted with language like this, may be inclined to clutch wildly at his hair and wonder if words in Portugal can possibly be thought to mean what they mean elsewhere.

Such are the difficulties. Official sources of information on matters that cannot reasonably be regarded as secrets of State, though they have often seemed to be so regarded in Portugal, have remained mute or closed. Not even Portugal's accession to the United Nations reduced the administrative silence. For when Portugal was duly admitted in 1955, its government at once denied that Articles such as Number 73, concerning non-self-governing territories, had any application to the new member, because the new member possessed no such territories. Strongly worked objections to this denial pointed to Portugal's undoubted possession of large territories in Africa as well as smaller ones elsewhere. To these objections the Portuguese Government replied that those territories were not non-self-governing, much less colonial, but overseas provinces of the motherland and constitutionally a part of Portugal itself.

This might seem another statement of the peculiar quality quoted already from Dr Franco Nogueira; constitutionally, however, it was true. An amendment to the Portuguese Constitution, made during 1951 in a period when Dr Salazar's régime was expecting to be admitted to the United Nations, had erased the word 'colonies' and replaced it with the term 'overseas provinces'. Hence there could be no good reason, it was forthwith argued, for the United Nations to expect any action under Article 73, or under any other relevant provision of the Charter. Those who disagreed, and there were many who did, went on in their turn to point out that this verbal change had brought no other changes in its wake, and that these territories—in this context, Angola, Guinea, Mozambique, and Portugal's various offshore African islands—remained in practice just what they had been before in name as well, and were colonies in every real particular. It was an argument that Lisbon preferred not to hear or at least not to acknowledge having heard.

All this helps to explain the problems of discovering the reality of 'Portuguese Africa'. So far as the United Nations are concerned, the Portuguese authorities would accept absolutely no obligation to report on the territories that were colonies before 1951, and 'overseas provinces' thereafter. Other forms of inquiry, meanwhile, have been generally much confined by official discouragement in Lisbon and in Africa, the Portuguese Government evidently taking the view that nothing more could reasonably be required than their own periodical statements on the subject; the bare framework of official statistics, gravely deficient in detail though these usually are; and reassurances from visitors favourable to their point of view. One may add at this point that these circumstances throw into its full light the important initiative that Unesco has taken in promoting and publishing the remarkable and timely report which follows here.

As matters stood in the second half of the 1950s, this poverty of detailed and reliable information on the huge expanses of Africa covered by Angola, Guinea and Mozambique (not to speak of the offshore islands), seemed likely to continue. But events since then have combined greatly to alter the situation. The most influential of these events, up to 1974 and the consequences of the *coup d'état* of 25 April, have been the growth and emergence on the public scene of nationalist movements which took their rise in a necessary clandestinity and illegality during the 1950s. These movements have of course remained illegal under Portuguese law which regarded them as criminal organizations, fit only for repression by the police, long before they embraced the strategies of armed resistance to colonial rule. They themselves have replied that they are fully legal in the eyes of all those who accept the right of Africans in 'Portuguese Africa' to the same equality and independence as all other peoples who have emerged from foreign domination. This claim to a real and natural legality has been widely accepted, and even before 1974 the movements were already accorded the recognition of consultative status in the organs of the United Nations. They were thus accepted as the rightful precursors of independent organs of countries which could in due course become Member States of the United Nations.

These developments have greatly helped to improve the flow of detailed information about the everyday lives and means of livelihood, experiences and intentions, self-organization and cultural condition of the Africans of these colonies. Hence it comes about that some 15 million people have found authentic voices of their own, speaking for about 6 million people in Angola, about 8 million in Mozambique, about 1 million in Guinea and the historically related islands of the Cape Verde archipelago, together with small populations in the islands of Saõ Tomé, Príncipe and other offshore fragments of the Portuguese empire. Many observers from countries of widely varying political complexions have been able to visit and travel extensively in areas of these colonies from which the nationalists have removed all control by the Portuguese armed forces.

At the same time, a great deal more of world attention has become focused on the material and other consequences of Portuguese colonial policy, whether social or cultural, political or military; and in this respect the Secretariat of the United Nations has continuously played a key role in the publication of reports of the General Assembly and of other United Nations bodies concerned with non-self-governing peoples, human rights, labour conditions, and other matters which fall within their purview. These reports already form a body of evidence of considerable factual value to the researcher, and indeed to anyone who should wish to arrive at objective judgements in this great and painful issue.

The circumstances of nationalist emergence are now well known, and here need be sketched only in brief outline. Up to 1961 it was claimed for the Portuguese régime that its special virtue had made it exempt from those demands for African progress and equality which all other colonies had known in Africa. Unprejudiced observers of these territories found the claim hard or impossible to accept; during 1961, in any case, it was revealed as manifestly baseless. Nationalist risings in western and northern Angola during the early months of the year shattered the official picture of sweetness and light. African nationalist movements had appealed for political change. Their appeals had been met with increased repression by the police. Thus denied, they now turned to methods of counter-violence as being the sole means that remained to these populations of achieving the recognition of their own identity and of their right to rule themselves. Tired of being 'auxiliaries' a status which they felt in practice as being little different from a modern serfdom, they wished to be masters in their own lands.

Almost at once it became clear on the public scene that the same processes were far advanced in Guinea and in Mozambique. There, too, the nationalists had appealed to Lisbon for peaceful change; and there, too, once this appeal proved vain, they now turned to self-defence by other means. Just as the Angolan nationalist movement, the MPLA (Movimento Popular de Libertação de Angola), had led the way in February 1961, so now did the PAIGC (Partido Africano da Independencia da Guiné e Cabo Verde) declare armed resistance to colonial rule in January 1963, and FRELIMO (Frente de Libertação de Moçambique) in September 1964.

Relevant here is the manner in which all this has built towards a better flow of detailed information. To begin with, the few and lonely African voices of the 1950s have become many, and these have spoken with an increasing confidence and authority. What they have had to say, moreover, has also widened steadily across the whole spectrum of social life. It is important for us to understand why this has happened, and how it has become possible. The answers lie in the work accomplished in areas liberated from foreign rule.

Though with many setbacks, ups downs and difficulties imposed by the nature of their task as well as by a vast military effort to eliminate them, the nationalist movements had by 1974 brought extensive areas under their influence or control. Little by little, within these areas, and with an obviously varying degree of intensity according to the hazards of an ever-shifting military situation, these Africans had begun to anticipate national independence by promoting the institutions of a new society within which their peoples could forge a genuine sovereignty and common purpose.

Conceived as the basic organs of an independent national unity and consciousness, these new institutions transcend both the ethnic separatism of African tradition and the racist separatism of colonial rule. They have matured in a number of significant ways. Each of these ways has helped to illuminate the old realities within which these peoples have lived and to explain the new realities within which they begin to live now, as well as the further aims for which they work and resist. Their basis lies in a democratically structured network of committees of local self-rule within the new unities and consciousness of a progressive nationalism.

These village committees of local self-rule were not easy to establish, as much of the evidence suggests, but have gradually achieved a representative character and even, in the more advanced areas, a fully elective character. Here, indeed, one evidently finds an important bridge between traditional modes of village government in the precolonial centuries and modernizing modes of today. Scattered through woodland and plains, dense forest or swampy seaboards, these highly localized committees in areas liberated from colonial rule are linked, in turn, to sector committees and to larger organs of a similar nature.

So far has this process of restructuring been carried that it became possible during 1972 for the PAIGC in Guinea to promote a general election throughout wide-ranging liberated areas. Conducted by direct and secret ballot after a prolonged campaign of political education and explanation, this general consultation duly elected fifteen regional committees. These proceeded to elect a National Assembly with the primary task of proclaiming the sovereignty and independence of this new State of independent Guinea; even while the capital of Bissau and some part of the national territory were still held by the Portuguese armed forces.

This political advance in areas liberated from the Portuguese has gone together with the installation of elementary social services in the measure of the possible, notably for education, public health and the administration of an independent code of law. In other words, the old has given way to the new even while the wars have continued; and the 'auxiliaries' of yesterday, however hard-pressed by hunger and a manifestly acute shortage of every means of material advance, have begun to forge for themselves a practical freedom they had not known before. A full review of all this must obviously await another volume of inquiry and an appropriately detailed documentation. Here it may be enough to note that many independent observers have borne witness to the nature of life in these liberated areas, whether in Angola, Guinea or Mozambique; and this work of observation was crowned in 1972 by the visit to Guinea of a team of observers from the United Nations itself.[1]

1. A/AC. 109/1804 of 3 July 1972: *Report of the Special Mission . . .*

Meanwhile, in the light of much new information accumulated over the past few years, and as a means of indicating the special values of Dr Ferreira's report, one may briefly consider the recent evolution of Portuguese colonial policy, and of nationalist responses to this evolution. The consequences of each of these aspects of the drama now confront the history of our times, and stand upon the centre of the stage.

Though former Foreign Minister Franco Nogueira might claim for Portugal's 'overseas provinces' a condition 'more developed, more progressive in every respect than any recently independent territory in Africa south of the Sahara, without exception', it none the less appeared in 1961 that they were not quite perfect. Reacting to world-wide criticism after the risings of that year in Angola and their massive repression at the cost of many thousands of African lives, perhaps more than 20,000 on the evidence of Christian missionary sources present at the time, Lisbon responded with further constitutional reforms.

Two of these reforms deserve mention. Both offer an interesting commentary on Dr Nogueira's claim that Portugal has 'practised the principle of multi-racialism . . . the most perfect and daring expression of human brotherhood'. One was the formal abolition of long-established systems of 'contract labour' which had evolved from the period of outright slavery and colonial *mise en valeur*. These systems were widely accused of a barely trammelled coercion and a scarcely more concealed abuse, and long-standing African resentment against 'the contract' provided a central motive in the risings of 1961. So far as coercion was concerned, the 'contract' was accompanied by the imposing of an obligation on African farmers to cultivate certain cash crops, such as cotton, for purchase by European buyers at prices fixed by European buyers. Here, too, there was some relaxation after 1961.

A second constitutional change was the formal abolition of the differential statuses of *assimilado* and *indígena*. Up to 1961, in spite of the 'most perfect and daring expression of human brotherhood and sociological progress', the populations of these territories were legally and rigidly divided into two kinds of people: those enjoying the constitutional rights and privileges of Portuguese citizens, however restricted these might be by the authoritarian principles of the régime, and those enjoying none of these rights and privileges. And in 1961 the proportion of Africans in the first category, after some five centuries of Portuguese presence along the coasts of these lands and some seventy years of the aforesaid 'expression of human brotherhood', remained extremely small.

Exact figures are hard to fix. Yet the proportion of *assimilados* in Angola may have been about 2 per cent, rather less in Mozambique, and very much less again in Guinea, where it was practically invisible. (The offshore islands, whether those of Cape Verde or of São Tomé and Príncipe, were somewhat different). All constitutional and other verbal assurances to the contrary, the vast majority of these populations were thus subject to a constitutional and customary discrimination essentially no different, in its everyday effect and the working of the laws, from South African apartheid.

How far such reforms have become real, or could become real in the circumstances, remains a question for further study; but it is one of the values of Dr Ferreira's report that much of its evidence bears upon the answer. What is beyond question, in any case, is that the situation within Portuguese-controlled areas after these reforms stayed fully within the Portuguese colonial tradition and doctrine as set forth by the late Dr Salazar, by former Prime Minister Caetano, and by other luminaries of the past régime such as Dr da Silva Cunha, former Overseas Minister and a noted authority on Portuguese colonial labour law.[1] Social, cultural or political advance for Africans as *Africans* was admitted as being possible no more than before. If there was to be advance for them, they must become Portuguese. On all this, too, Dr Ferreira's study has much to say of interest.

Effective or not, the post-1961 reforms did not take place in a vacuum. The Angolan risings were crushed with what may be described as an extreme severity: even so, the resistance continued, and was soon joined by other resistances of the same nature (if with many local variations) in Guinea and then in Mozambique. They were met by colonial warfare on a rising scale of destruction of people and property, and an ever-greater dislocation of social life. This failed to overcome or even to contain a continuously widening resistance, as the facts amply show, so that by 1972 there was no exaggeration in saying that these wars had become the longest and largest that Africa has ever had to suffer.

1. See especially J. M. da Silva Cunha, *O Sistema Portugues de Politica Indigena*, Coimbra, 1953. There, among other things, it is made doctrinally clear that civilization in Africa is to be regarded as equivalent, and only as equivalent, to assimilation to European cultures, in this case to Portuguese culture.

By the beginning of the 1970s the Portuguese were thought to have committed to these wars a total metropolitan force, aside from local levies, of perhaps 130,000 men on a probable maximum possible conscription of all men of fighting age. Some notion of the relative size of these forces may be had from comparing them on a *per capita* basis of population with, for example, the forces sent by the United States to the Republic of Viet-Nam. The population of the United States of America being about twenty-five times larger than the population of Portugal, these forces in Africa represent a Portuguese effort that would be equivalent to a United States army in the Republic of Viet-Nam of about 3,250,000 men, or more than six times the largest force of American troops in the Republic of Viet-Nam at the height of that war.

Everything in history suggests that progressive reforms of social and cultural structure, let alone political structure, can never be carried through effectively in the midst of warfare, and certainly not of a warfare as intensive as this. Whatever improvements Portuguese sincerity may have wished to dictate after 1961, reality was now in the hands of military need. Increasingly through the 1960s, this yielded a contradiction familiar from other countries in a comparable situation.

On one hand, it was seen that some large effort must be made to improve the lot of the African populations, especially of rural Africans who form their great majority, if only to counter the appeal and attraction exercised by the movements of national liberation. There should be a genuine attempt to revise the laws that governed African life, and to provide the schools, clinics and other civilized facilities which Portuguese rule, *pace* Dr Nogueira, had evidently not provided or thought it useful to provide.

Yet all such reforms, in so far as money was available to pay for them at a time when the wars were absorbing nearly half the Portuguese national budget and a sizeable proportion of the overseas budgets, had to be introduced *manu militari*, and the military, for reasons mandatory from their point of view, such as the requirements of counter-insurgency, were bound to have other priorities in mind. Thus the considerable administrative effort devoted to such reforms, for example in central Angola, has found itself repeatedly contradicted by the needs of military action. As examples from elsewhere have often shown, the contradiction is all too likely to be a fatal one.

An attempt was made to resolve this contradiction by

adopting the policy of concentrating rural people within militarily controlled villages or settlements. First applied in Angola during the early 1960s, this policy appeared in rural Guinea and Mozambique in areas where the Portuguese army could still exercise a sufficient control, and, most recently, in the contested District of Tete of central Mozambique. Very large numbers of village cultivators, and sometimes of semi-nomad pastoralists, were removed from their homes and habitats, and driven into more or less large concentrations under military supervision. These concentrations were supposed to receive schools and clinics, and the extent to which they have really done so is another point related to Dr Ferreira's evidence. Yet the trouble has remained that these concentrations are in no sense places of free assembly or residence, or of free movement between them, and are subject to the abuses and repression that must always occur in such enterprises.[1]

For one reason or another, and very probably also for this reason of far-reaching social dislocation and its consequences, the movements of national liberation have continued to grow in strength, reinforcing their resistance and widening their operations, drawing more and more people into active participation in their struggle. At least since 1966 they proved able on the military side to improve their tactics, acquire and use better weapons, enlarge their units, and press more strongly on Portuguese fortified positions and lines of communication. In areas normally under their firm protection, they meanwhile continued with their work of promoting the institutions of a new society. On their side the Portuguese scored military gains from time to time, but these could not reserve the trend against them.

In these circumstances the Portuguese authorities came gradually to the conclusion, beginning in Guinea during 1968, that they must add political warfare to military repression. To that end they began to embark on other reforms. Constitutional changes were proposed in 1971 which duly gave the oversea provinces the faculty of calling themselves, if they wished, 'autonomous provinces' or even 'autonomous States'; which enlarged the advisory legislatures of each of the overseas territories and encouraged the election of black candidates; and which, in various ways, gave a new emphasis to the policies of

---

1. Much documented: E. G. J. Hoagland, *Washington Post*, 14 March 1971; G. Bender in *Journal of Comparative Politics* (United States), Vol. IV, No. 3, 1972; detailed evidence of Portuguese army massacres provided by missionary sources and widely published in July 1973; and much else to the same effect.

amelioration enunciated some years earlier. Elections to these legislatures were duly conducted during 1973, and produced, in the case of Mozambique, a majority of black members.

This shift in tactics was accompanied by others of the same nature. Moving towards positions comparable with those of some British and French African colonies after 1945, Lisbon opened a number of senior administrative posts to assimilated 'natives', while the Portuguese army, now finding it hard to reinforce its white effectives, began a new effort to recruit and commit African troops by outright conscription or the offer of relatively high pay and at least a second-class military status.[1]

With all this there now began to be sketched, at least in the more imaginative or inflated of official statements, a picture of 'overseas provinces' which would gradually grow into 'autonomous States' along with the admission, made for the first time, that these provinces of Portugal might just possibly be African countries as well. Yet what reality could be discerned behind these shifts in the scenery?

They were not, as subsequent events were to prove in 1974, in any case, more than shifts of scenery, nor were presented as being more, at least in texts intended to be taken seriously. The constitutional amendments allowed for no devolution of power from Lisbon whose then Overseas Minister, the veteran Dr da Silva Cunha, continued as before to control all matters of substance, as well as all appointments in the administative services, whether directly or indirectly through his governors, who remained his appointees.

The possibility that one or other of these territories might call itself an 'autonomous State' likewise made no change; to quote a semi-official Coimbra commentary:

> . . . the legislative, executive and judicial organs of each province express no sovereignty other than that of the Portuguese nation as a whole, which, above all, is manifested or exercised as far as the Constitution is concerned through the formulation of a simple constitution. . . . An entity

1. In 1971 the Portuguese army in Guinea included about 4,000 African troops, as well as another 4,000 in para-military militias, according to Lt-Col. Lemos Pires, a principal aid of the Governor and Commanding General, in conversation with the white South African journalist, A. J. Venter (cf. Venter's *Portugal's War in Guinea-Bissau*, p. 50, California Institute of Technology, 1973). Portuguese metropolitan troops in Guinea, according to the same source, numbered 30,000. Comparable figures for Angola and Mozambique have been generally given as considerably higher by all competent sources.

lacking in constituent power is not a sovereign entity and is not, legally speaking, a state.[1]

Whether in principle or practice, the approach was clearly the reverse of those ideas which led to internal self-government of Ghana and Nigeria in the British African empire in 1951 and after, and to similar changes expressed by the *loi cadre* of 1956 in the French African empire. These gestures are to be swept away in the democratic optique of 1974. In fact, they represented little more than counter-nationalist political warfare, and, even so, met with severe criticism from influential groups in Portugal as well as from settler groups in Africa, though not exactly for the same reasons. The critics in Portugal evidently feared that any concessions to African advancement would undermine the structure of the Portuguese empire. The settlers might care little for the Portuguese empire, and even deplore its existence in the manner of Rhodesia's white settlers *vis à vis* Rhodesia's colonial status; but their spokesmen have appeared unanimous—even in 1974—in saying that any devolution of power from Lisbon must be to their own sectional advantage rather than to that of the Africans.

What is obviously of crucial significance, in this context, is the judgement and estimate of the movements of national liberation. For their part and from the very first, and increasingly over the past three years, these movements have rejected any solution which should rest upon a compromise with the Portuguese colonial system. They have set forth their reasons at considerable length and on many occasions, notably in preliminary talks with the new Portuguese régime after April 1974, and here these reasons must be at least briefly resumed.

They point out, to begin with, that any such reforms were without any real substance, as indeed serious Portuguese texts likewise admit. But they go on to state that even if such reforms were to be carried into real effect they could yield no more than a façade of autonomy, much less a genuine independence, unless this were to be an autonomy or independence in which, at least for Angola and Mozambique, local white settler populations would achieve a mastery comparable with that exercised in Rhodesia. But they also go further than this; and it is on this further and essential argument against comprise with colonial structures that Dr Ferreira's study, as will be seen, acquired a further explanatory value, especially in the light of the 1974 *coup d'état*.

1. From the report of a special constitutional committee, quoted here from *West Africa*, 23 June 1972, p. 791.

The essence of this further argument is that no reform of existing structures, whether of colonial rule or of such traditional ways of life as may have survived the colonial dismantlement, can now enable these African populations to realize their own identity, develop their own cultures and economies, and exercise their own rights. Only a new society, such as they are striving to build in their liberated areas, can do that. Within existing structures, however much modified by constitutional reform, Africans would remain 'auxiliaries', directly or indirectly, and could purchase a primary role, if at all, only by the abandonment of their own identities and cultures in favour of those of the Portuguese.

Thinking thus, they have repeatedly made it clear that they are not fighting a war against Portugal, or against the Portuguese as a people, and are willing to negotiate a friendly solution so long as it recognizes the fullness of African self-determination and sovereignty.

But the last point, the recognition of their full sovereignty within a non-racist and non-discriminatory independence, is not negotiable for them. And it cannot be negotiable for them, since to concede on this decisive point would be to cast away their work for a new society. But in casting that away they would renounce the moral and social justification for their struggle with all the sufferings it has imposed.

How determined has become this rejection of comprise on the basic issue can be fully understood, no doubt, only by a full consideration of their liberated areas. Yet the understanding will emerge even from a rapid survey of the evidence, for it is here, in these liberated areas, that the inner meanings of the word 'liberation' are immediately present for inspection. This conception, it there appears, is one of a human emancipation that implies much more than the removal of foreign rule, but goes towards the freeing of creative energies and talents through a victory, however hardly won, over ignorance and illiteracy, technological backwardness and all the mystifications of racist or 'tribalist' confusion. The aim here is to win through to a real unity by way of a real participation; and this unity is to be used in the service of new communities capable of progress and internal peace. All this embodies what Amilcar Cabral has called 'a forced march on the road to cultural progress.[1]

This march has now gone beyond the realm of mere aspiration.

1. A. Cabral, 'National Liberation and Culture', lecture delivered at Syracuse University, New York, 20 February 1970.

Cabral told the Fourth Commission of the United Nations in October 1972, speaking for his own country but undoubtedly for his colleagues of the MPLA and FRELIMO as well:

> For the people of Guinea and Cape Verde and their national party . . . the greatest success of their struggle did not lie in the fact that they had fought victoriously against the Portuguese colonialist troops under extremely difficult conditions, but rather the fact that, while they were fighting, they had begun to create all the aspects of a new life—political, administrative, economic, social and cultural—in the liberated areas.
>
> The nearly 10 years of struggle had not only forged a new, strong African nation but also created a new man and a new woman, people possessing an awareness of their rights and duties on the soil of the African fatherland. Indeed, the most important result of the struggle, which was at the same time its greatest strength, was the new awareness of the country's men, women and children. The people of Guinea and Cape Verde did not take any great pride in the fact that every day, because of circumstances created and imposed by the Government of Portugal, an increasing number of young Portuguese were dying ingloriously before the withering fire of the freedom-fighters.
>
> What filled them with pride was their ever-increasing national consciousness, their unity—now indestructible—which had been forged in war, the harmonious development and coexistence of the various cultures and ethnic groups, the schools, hospitals and health centres which were operating openly in spite of the bombs and the terrorist attacks of the Portuguese colonialists, the people's stores which were increasingly able to supply the needs of the population, the increase and qualitative improvement in agricultural production, and the beauty, pride and dignity of their children and their women, who were the most exploited human beings in the country. . . .[1]

The aims and achievements of these nationalist movements in their liberated areas demonstrate what may be said to be the positive aspect of their rejection of any mere reform of the structures and institutions of colonial rule, and thus of any formula for 'autonomy'

1. General Assembly A/C.4/SR.1986 of 19 October 1972.

within the Portuguese system, or indeed any other system of foreign control. But these movements have also adduced another category of reasons for this rejection. These arise especially in the cultural and social fields. Even if foreign political control were to be removed, what social and cultural institutions or structures within the Portuguese system can be usefully reformed in the service of new nations seeking unity and freedom?

The liberation movements have attentively examined this question, and have been better placed to do so than anyone else, for they know the Portuguese system from within but also from 'below', as anyone who cares to study the copious documentation now available will quickly be convinced. And the answer they have reached is invariably negative. Little that now exists within the Portuguese system can be usefully reformed; and even this little can be usefully reformed only within the institutions of an African society entirely different from any conceived by the doctrine of imperial Portugal.

The Portuguese themselves, one may note, have repeatedly pointed out to the same conclusion. In the matter of educational policy, for example, nothing has changed in the assimilationist principles adopted before the wars began. What those principles were may be seen from a Christmas message of 1960 from Lisbon's Patriarch, Cardinal Cerejeira, one of the most respected and authoritative pillars of the régime.

> We need schools in Africa, but schools in which we show the native the way to the dignity of man and the glory of the Nation that protects him.

And to make it quite clear what this 'way' really implied, and where it really led to, the Cardinal went on to add:

> We want to teach the natives to write, to read and to count, but not make them doctors.[1]

Quoted by Mr Ferreira in his careful and objective study of the cultural parameters of Portuguese rule, Cardinal Cerejeira's definition of what schools should do for Africans, and of what they should not do, is merely an indication, though a useful one, of the reality of cultural deformation and deprivation imposed by existing institutions.

1. Page 113; see also pages 66–73,

The national liberation movements have studied this reality in its every manifestation, and have reached their conclusions.

This is a reality that they know from the experience and travail of their own lives, a reality composed of an endless elaboration of detail. Their convictions and their struggle express the judgements they have made. But what judgements can be reached from a study of the available statistical record, enlightened and explained by the whole panoply of official and semi-official texts and glosses? This is the question that Unesco asked Mr Ferreira to approach and answer. It was no easy task. The records are scattered and diffuse, often hard to find, sometimes impossible to find. The statistics are notoriously defective. Yet the author persevered in his pioneering investigation. What he gives us here, beyond any doubt, is a document of the highest value, a milestone in the study of this whole subject, a clearly factual point of orientation, a penetratingly objective view of the landscape as it really is.

This study was useful before the *coup d'état* of 25 April 1974, and its liberating consequences. Today, in the wake of that change and all it has meant and is likely to mean, Dr Ferreira's work acquires a programmatic significance it could not have before. Here, as it were, is the basic cultural and educational agenda of initiative and reconstruction to which these peoples, unhampered by colonial war, now become free to turn their attention.

BASIL DAVIDSON
London, 1 September 1974

I Portuguese colonialism: a historical introduction

1 Background

Portugal formerly proclaimed that, during the five centuries in which it dominated African territories, it was engaged in a civilizing mission. This was taken as legitimizing its presence in Africa in our own times and its determination to continue holding colonial peoples under its political control.

One aspect of its alleged civilizing mission is examined below: the history of education in its colonies during the centuries. A glance at history furthermore reveals that Portuguese sovereignty was for long sporadic, and limited to points scattered along the African coast. From their first appearance in the fifteenth century in Africa until the nineteenth century, the Portuguese presence consisted mainly of slave and gold traders, and a small number of missionaries. It was estimated that, 300 years after the nominal installation of Portuguese sovereignty in Angola, 'less than one-tenth of the territory within the colony's official borders'[1] was under effective control; and, in the middle of the nineteenth century, there were only 1,832 whites in Angola and Benguela.[2]

Increased Portuguese settlement and increased administrative control of the territories that make up the present colonies did not start before the 1850s and were not systematically organized until after the Berlin Conference (1884–85). Apart from the fact that Europeans had not acquired the same immunity to tropical diseases as the indigenous population, the belated generalization of the Portuguese occupation can be attributed mainly to two factors.

First, Portugal, because of the permanent resistance, had establish-

---

1. John Marcum, *The Angolan Revolution*. Vol. I: *The Anatomy of an Explosion (1950–1962)*, p. 3, Cambridge, Mass, and London, 1969.
2. Lopes de Lima, *Ensaios sobre a Estatística das possessões portuguezas, Livro III*, Lisbon, 1846.

ed footholds, protected by fortresses, along the coast, but had not been able to penetrate inland. Queen Jinga—although she had consented to the slave trade as practised by the Portuguese—became a symbol of Angolan resistance. The fact that, at the end of the seventeenth century, de Cadornega set out to write a three-volume general history of the wars of Angola serves to indicate that there was an abundance of material on the subject. The Berlin Conference invited Portugal to prove her effective control over the colonial territories claimed. In trying to impose such control, Portugal had to face strong resistance from the African populations. In Angola, the wars of conquest lasted from 1906 to 1919, thirteen years of heavy fighting and bloodshed. In Mozambique, Enes and Albuquerque conquered the Gaza area in the south in 1896 and the 'pacification' of the north was completed in 1904. With the defeat of the Mokombe (King) of Barwe in 1918, the armed resistance was broken. In Guinea-Bissau, Portugal fought for thirty years against the animists. Between 1913 and 1915 there were four wars of conquest; while the archipelago of Bijagos was brought under Portuguese control only in 1936.

The second factor lay in the peculiar economic features of Portuguese colonialism. Merchants were allowed to trade only on behalf of the Crown which laid down conditions regarding times and prices which deprived them of economic initiative. They became a commercial aristocracy, adopted feudal ways, and depended exclusively on trade instead of making investments and helping to establish industries —the stage through which other colonial powers passed on their way to industrial capitalism. These other powers were exporting manufactures and so reinforcing their economics. Portugal failed to meet this competition. Brazilian independence (1822) and the abolition of the slave trade (1840) caused a crisis which led to her being replaced in trade by Holland and later by England.

Only then did interest shift to the Portuguese settlement of the African colonies.[1] However, Angola was still not effectively occupied. The Commercial Association of Luanda reported that, in the last quarter of the nineteenth century, the colony was still short of 'centres of permanent civilized [i.e. white] population'. In other words, Portugal's failure to industrialize made her incapable of competing with the other colonial powers. Her presence in Africa was not

3. Ilidio do Amaral, *Aspectos do Povoamento de Angola, Junta de Investigaçoes do Ultramar*, p. 16, Lisbon, 1960.

explained by her need to expand (as in the case of the other colonial powers) but, on the contrary, the result of her underdeveloped economy which needed colonial profits to maintain her position.

At the Berlin Conference, Portugal's claim to her African colonies was supported by Britain: in view of the explorations undertaken by Brazza for the French and Stanley for the Belgian governments, Britain feared a curtailment of her influence in Africa, and wanted to abate this danger by strengthening the Portuguese position. Besides, Britain regarded the Portuguese territories more or less as her own because of Portugal's weakness and semi-colonial dependence on Britain.

However, the Berlin Conference made effective occupation the vital condition. Portugal was forced, for the first time, to exercise systematic control and expand the Portuguese presence in Africa. By 1897, 9,000 Portuguese were living in Angola, a large increase since the middle of the century. Nevertheless Ilídio do Amaral wrote that, at the beginning of the twentieth century, the Portuguese had to organize campaigns of pacification to subdue indigenous potentates who, in constant revolt, endangered the harmony, organization and colonization of the province.[1]

The colonies of the industrialized powers were a kind of natural prolongation of the home countries: although less developed, their economies represented an embryonic form of industrial capitalism. Economic underdevelopment at home (as in Portugal) means, on the contrary, that the possession of colonies is vital to the home economy, until such time as the metropolis undergoes changes that alter political conditions both in Portugal and in the colonies.[2]

The colonies played a particular and very important role in the Portuguese economy. First, they provided a protected market, supplying raw materials at prices cheaper than the world market rates and buying Portuguese products for which, in general, foreign demand is low. Secondly, their foreign exchange earnings from exports and services alleviated the chronic deficit on Portugal's balance of trade.

To safeguard these advantages, the Portuguese colonialist minority in the colonies had to be protected against possible African competition by economic segregation, and the white population was accord-

---

1. Relatório da Associaçaõ Comercial de Luanda, *Boletim Oficial da Colonia de Angola*, No. 33, *Suplemento*, 1887.
2. Do Amaral, op. cit., p. 20.

ingly concentrated in the cities or places of decisive economic importance.[1]

Portugal had at her disposal a labour force of many millions of Africans after the abolition of slavery, but failed to increase labour productivity by paying wages to free workers, as the other colonial countries did, and remained dependent on compulsory labour. The consequences, to this day, have been devastating for the African peoples.

A special representative of the then Portuguese Government, Henrique Galvão, at the end of the fifties, prepared a comprehensive report on the social conditions in the colonies; more recently, Basil Davidson, in his book on Angola, showed the extent to which they relied on compulsory labour.[2]

1. See Eduardo de Sousa Ferreira, *Portuguese Colonialism from South Africa to Europe*, p. 19–39, Freiburg, 1972.
2. See Henrique de Galvaõ de Carlos Salvagem, *Império Ultramarino Português*, Lisbon, 1950, and Basil Davidson, *In the Eye of the Storm: Angola's People*, London, 1972

2 Reforms

In the fifties and sixties, three factors helped to bring about a change in traditional Portuguese colonialism. First, a general anti-colonialist feeling grew up as a result of economic and political developments in Western industrial countries. Portugal, attempting to justify her presence in Africa, was forced to introduce at least certain nominal reforms. Secondly, armed revolts offered Africans an alternative to the acceptance of Portuguese domination, and again some reforms were introduced in the hope of counteracting the attraction of the liberation movements. Thirdly, in Portugal itself during the sixties, industrial interests began to compete for the political influence which had hitherto been an agrarian monopoly. The need for a less restricted economy, new labour techniques and increased productivity demanded changes both at home and in the formerly inflexible economic and social structures of the colonies.

One of Portugal's first reactions to the anti-colonialist movement was to pass a degree in 1955 regulating the use of compulsory labour for public works; it inflicted heavier penalties on the use of compulsory labour for private purposes, a practice abolished by law in 1928. This measure was meant to reassure world opinion. In reality, in 1958, 120,000 Africans were still conscripted in Angola, and 95,000 of them were working for private employers. In 1956, 500,000 Africans of Mozambique were forced to work on the cotton farms;[1] each received an average of $11.17 as payment for a year's work for himself and his family.[2]

Africans not called upon to do forced labour were discriminated

1. United Nations, *A Principle in Torment, II*, New York, 1970.
2. Martin Harris, *Portugal's African Wards*, New York, 1958.

TABLE 1. Wages of skilled workers in Angola (1958) (in escudos)

	Europeans	'Natives'		Europeans	'Natives'
Compositors, manual	4,500	1,560	Office workers	2,500	1,800
Carpenters	3,120	1,690	Stokers	4,000	450
Cooks	3,334	500	Drivers of		
Servants	1,500	450	light vehicles	2,500	1,200

Source: *Anuário Estatístico de Angola 1958*, Luanda.

against by being paid considerably lower wages for their work than whites.

Portugal was sufficiently impressed by the armed revolt in Angola in 1962 to abolish all forms of forced labour. The abolition was in name only. In 1969, Dr Afonso Mendes was asked for a confidential report suggesting ways in which the government could reduce Angolan support for the liberation movements. At the time, Dr Mendes was director of the Labour Institute which enforced legislation, grants licences to recruiters and generally regulated all labour conditions in Angola. The Mendes report stated that as long as employers continue to have recourse to professional recruiters and contract workers, no marked improvement could be expected in working conditions or in relations between employers and employees. Defence reasons were used as a pretext for obstacles imposed by both civil and military and para-military authorities. Repression was frequently used against workers at the request of individual employers by police and para-military authorities, and did not exclude extreme physical violence. In legal terms, all this came under the designation of forced labour.[1]

Dr Mendes also referred to discrimination with respect to payment for non-compulsory labour, and the large gap between the wages of the African worker and the worker of European origin: the average monthly wage of rural and assimilated workers (three-quarters of all workers), who are always of African origin, was 600 escudos; urban workers, predominantly of European origin, got six times that figure.[2]

1. *Petition by the Angola Comité concerning the Report by Mr Pierre Juvigny Regarding the Implementation of the Abolition of Forced Labour Convention, 1957 (No. 105) by Portugal*, p. 14–15. Directed to the International Labour Organisation, Geneva. Amsterdam, 1972.
2. ibid, p. 14.

In 1960, minimum wages were established by law, but low as they were, were not applied in practice. Minimum wage levels in force in 1965 varied between $34 and $204 per month for workers not entitled to extensive allowances (almost entirely urban semi-skilled and skilled workers), and between $23 and $75 (depending on district) plus housing, food, medical care, insurance, transport, schools, canteens and other allowances. The monthly rural wage actually paid for unskilled labour in Angola was on the average $7.50 in cash and $11.60 in allowances, totalling $19.10 per month. In Mozambique, rural salaries, including allowances, for unskilled daily labour ranged from $8.80 to $17.20 per month, varying according to the district, and for industrial unskilled labour from $10.20 to $18.50.[1] In 1971, the minimum wages established by law in Angola were from 25 to 30 escudos per day. In the same year, the minimum wages for rural workers in Mozambique were 15 escudos per day in the northern districts, 19 escudos in the central districts and 22 escudos in the southern districts. As the employer was entitled to deduct up to 50 per cent for clothing, food and accommodation, the money income paid in the extreme case amounted to not more than 7.5 escudos per day.[2]

Secondly, as a reaction to the sympathy aroused among Africans to the liberation movements, Portugal abolished the distinction between 'civilized' and 'non-civilized'. The latter included almost all Africans (*indígenas*). They had no civil rights—with all the economic and social consequences that this implies, including eligibility for forced labour. The only exceptions were the *assimilados*, i.e. Africans who had broken with their traditional bonds and adapted themselves to the Portuguese language and culture. According to the 1950 census: of some 4 million Africans in Angola, only 30,089 had *assimilado* status; and of 5.7 million Africans in Mozambique, only 4,349. The distinction was now abolished, and all Africans were formally declared to be Portuguese citizens. The extent to which the declaration remained a formality is dealt with below in the chapter on culture.

The reforms introduced during the sixties culminated in the constitutional reform of 1971, which was said to give the colonies greater autonomy, even referring to Angola and Mozambique as 'States'. There had been one more change already, in 1951: the

1. See D. M. Abshire and M. A. Samuels (eds.), *Portuguese Africa. A Handbook*, p. 170–1. London and New York, 1969.
2. See Joachim F. Kahl, *Pro und kontra Portugal*, p. 141, Stuttgart, 1972.

colonies had been renamed Portuguese provinces to forestall United Nations intervention. The constitutional law relating to the colonies was revised in April 1972, and all colonies were given new statutes in December of the same year.

A rapid analysis of the constitutional reform will suffice to show that there was an adjustment to new conditions but that the change was purely superficial.[1] Article 133 of the revised constitution read:

> The territories of the Portuguese Nation outside Europe are the Overseas Provinces which, as autonomous regions, have their own constitutions and may, by national tradition, be called States if their degree of social progress and administrative complexity justifies this honorific title.

Nevertheless, the considerenda to the new law state that it does not introduce anything essentially new. In Article 136, the limitations on the autonomous regions are indicated:

> The exercise of autonomy by the Overseas Provinces shall not affect the unity of the Portuguese Nation and State power. In this regard it is the responsibility of the supreme State body
> (a) to represent the entire Nation at home and abroad; the Overseas Provinces shall not be permitted to maintain diplomatic or consular relations with foreign powers;
> (b) to enact laws on subjects of mutual interest or of supreme State interest . . . and to suspend or annul such local laws as may be in contradiction with these interests . . .
> (c) to nominate the Governor of each Province . . .
> (d) to supervise the administration of the Provinces . . .
> (e) to control the financial administration.

On the possibility of the colonies bearing the 'honorific title' of 'State', even the Portuguese Corporative Chamber voiced its scepticism:

> The legislative organs of the Overseas Provinces do not express the sovereign will of their populations; no local executive responsible to a legislative assembly which the peoples of the Overseas Provinces would consider, even indirectly, as their representative exists . . . no juridical power

---

1. See de Sousa Ferreira, op. cit., p. 149 et seq.

exists in the Overseas Provinces which is exercised solely by citizens originating from those Provinces. . . . It is likewise stated that the Bill uses the term 'State' in one of those figurative or metaphorical meanings. . . .

These extracts render commentary superfluous: the chamber made it perfectly clear that the constitutional revision made no change regarding the autonomy of the colonies. According to the constitution, moreover, it was Lisbon which decided whether or not the colonies had socially 'progressed'; and no change in the status of the colonies could be made in the metropolis while power was firmly in the hands of colonialists.

The number of deputies sent by the colonies to the Portuguese National Assembly was increased in 1971 from 23 to 43 (out of a total of 150 deputies). The National Assembly, under the régime of the Estado Novo, was merely acclamatory, and could make no major decisions. Hence the increased representation had no practical significance. Even so, it may be useful to consider how the colonial deputies represented the peoples of the colonies.

Since the abolition of the status of *indígena* in 1961 (see above), Africans and whites nominally enjoyed the same franchise. According to the electoral law of 1968, however, the right to vote could be exercised in the colonies only by people who could read and write Portuguese. As we shall see in the chapter on education, this in fact meant that only a very small proportion of Africans could vote. In the 1969 elections to the National Assembly, for example, the number was 82,539 in Mozambique, i.e. about 1 per cent of the population. The figures for Angola were not published; in the 1965 election, 3 per cent were entitled to vote. In other words, the franchise was confined almost entirely to whites, and African participation was practically non-existent.[1]

This affords clear evidence of the extent of exploitation and discrimination. The point is made unequivocally in the report of the Director of the Labour Institute, Dr Mendes, referred to above:

> Almost all the wealth, all the positions of leadership, all the agricultural, livestock, industrial and commercial enterprises, and the real decision-making power will remain in the hands of the European segment of the population, which in 1970

1. Kahl, op. cit., p. 75–6.

will continue to form merely a small minority as has always been the case. The positions of leadership in the public administration in Angola are filled by this segment of the population as well.

This situation resulted in a striking economic inequality between the 'white group' and the 'black group'. This leads to social inequality and to the maintenance of cultural inequality.[1]

1. *Petition by the Angola Comité . . .*, op. cit., p. 10.

3 The liberation movements

The colonial peoples have never ceased to oppose exploitation. The 'pacification' campaigns at the beginning of the century did, it is true, succeed in breaking the armed resistance, but resistance nevertheless continued and has continued to grow since the foundation in 1926 of the Estado Novo that brought Salazar to power.

However, the centre of resistance shifted[1]

> from the traditional hierarchies, which became docile puppets of the Portuguese, to individuals and groups.

Portugal had created a very narrow African élite class of *assimilados* with privileges which allowed them to participate in the exploitation of their compatriots but who, at the same time, had to witness day by day the humiliating situation of other Africans, and brutal repression. It is not surprising, under these circumstances, that it was the educated *assimilados* who were to form a political opposition.

The Liga Africana, founded in 1920, included black and mulatto students. Its very existence represented a step forward, since it not only went beyond tribal thinking and spoke in terms of national unity, but insisted that it was necessary to work for the joint liberation of the three colonies: Angola, Guinea-Bissau and Mozambique. Here was one of the worries of colonialism: a policy of destroying autochthonic structures and ignoring the differences between peoples resulted in Africans, estranged from their own societies, thinking and acting in terms of national categories, and gradually merging into a united force against colonialism on a national level.

1. Eduardo Mondlane, *The Struggle for Mozambique*, p. 102, Harmondsworth, 1969 (Penguin African Library).

However, groups such as the Liga Africana were short-lived, and their effect was relatively small. Political awareness acquired real force only after the Second World War, the defeat of fascism, and the growth of a world-wide anti-colonial movement. Urban intellectuals in Africa were in favour of cultural rebellion and a stronger sense of nationalism, but established no real contact with the countryside; they were strong in the towns, where Portuguese culture prevailed, but not in the rural areas, where traditional cultures continued to survive. Not until the fifties and sixties did the African nationalists succeed in establishing real contacts with the masses. For years, demands had been advanced through such democratic channels as were available, but the negative attitude of Portugal to them discredited peaceful methods. Massacres took place in Baixa do Cassange in Angola, Pidjiguitti in Guinea-Bissau, and Mueda in Mozambique. Liberation movements were formed, and spent their first years preparing for armed struggle and explaining the need for it to the population. The training of leaders was particularly difficult since, under the Portuguese-Catholic education system, only a small number of *assimilados* were educated, and then only for minor social and economic posts.

Armed revolt began in Angola in 1961, spread to Guinea in 1963 and to Mozambique in 1964. Portugal responded by recruiting an army which accounted for 28.7 per cent of government expenditure in 1962, rising to 44.4 per cent in 1970 (9 per cent of the Gross Domestic Product).[1] Portugal received substantial support for these activities from Western industrial countries that had a major interest in the economic exploitation of the colonies and hence in supporting Portuguese efforts to maintain it; and also from the Republic of South Africa, whose very existence depends on having a strong white block in southern Africa.

However, the Portuguese troops were not able to prevent the liberation movements from gaining extended liberated areas.

> The liberated areas form . . . the frame for changes which are brought about by the practice of these popular wars. In the remote areas, where the population was exposed to the despotism of the colonial administration and did not know either school or hospital, a revolution takes place. . . .

1. Banco de Portugal, *Annual Reports*.

> Through the path of creative destruction, the rural popula-
> tion in particular, under the leadership of the political bodies
> of their organizations, make the experience of independence.[1]

Economically, socially and politically, the colonial structures were being attacked.

This armed struggle has brought something new to Black Africa. It is not only the colonialists who are being fought, but every kind of oppression, of exploitation of man by man. This prevents the danger of replacing colonialists by an autochthonic *bourgeoisie*, and to a continuation of oppression as has happened elsewhere under various forms of neo-colonialism.

Portugal was constantly forced to try to counteract the liberation movements by reforms that were in fact purely tactical measures. Their stated purpose—the advancement of the African population— would inevitably jeopardize the Portuguese dominance; a fact that was evident to people in the liberated areas in which the nationalist movements exercised *de facto* sovereignty.

1. Mário de Andrade, quoted in 'Afrique Portuguaise—autre Vietnam', *Frères du Monde* (Bordeaux), No. 68, 1970, p. 62–3.

II Education and science

1 The history of education

Portugal has represented a deep concern and great efforts to spread education among Africans as essential features of her colonial policy ever since the age of the 'discoveries'.

> It can thus be said that, in Angola, the task of education and assistance began with the first voyage of the Portuguese. It was not that we imposed it, the autochthonic populations absorbed it, assimilated it.[1]

Were the effects on education in the colonies clearly positive? Let us look at the history and recent past of the African territories of colonial powers.

The first contacts

Educational activities in the various areas corresponding approximately to the present Portuguese colonies in Africa began at different times and under different conditions.

Congo and present-day Angola

The first activity after the landing of Diogo Cão in Congo (the kingdom that extended along the two banks of the river Zaire) in 1483 was:

> . . . the institution of colonial traditions which continue to the present day. Here they find abundant historical example

1. Martins dos Santos, *História do Ensino em Angola*, p. 14, Angola, Ediçao dos Serviços de Educaçao, 1970.

for avowed sentiments of racial equality, for sincere attempts
to educate and Christianize the African—with the African's
consent—and for relatively disinterested economic and
military assistance.[1]

The first Africans to be educated in Lisbon were brought, not at
all voluntarily, to Portugal as hostages by Diogo Cão, whose com-
panions were retained at the Manicongo court because they were
mistrusted. These hostages were treated 'in a lordly manner'[2] and
sent by King João II to the Convent of Santo Elói for their education[3]
in furtherance of Portugal's aims: first, the conversion of the Manicongo (soon accomplished when King Nzinga Nkuwu became King
João in order to evangelize the Manicongo people, and so guarantee
Portugal's own favoured economic position); and secondly, to
establish liaison with the Ethiopian Kingdom of the supposedly
Christian Prester John.[4]

From his second voyage, Diogo Cão again brought Africans to
be educated in Lisbon, this time voluntarily. They were 'the sons
of the most powerful lords'[5] who, when educated, were intended
to take over the administration and serve as intermediaries for
Portugal—hardly evidence of an intention to generalize education. . . .

To win Portuguese support, the King of the Congo asked Portugal
to send out priests and skilled workers. Manuel I sent some missionaries and technicians who proved to be of little service because they
were very inefficient.

> The incompetence of the Portuguese artisans is difficult to
> explain, and can perhaps be attributed to the difficulty of
> exercising a specialized craft in a strange milieu.[6]

> . . . This explanation is not very convincing. The Portuguese
> sent specialists into other strange places and their achieve-
> ments still outline them. Did they send only bad artisans,
> or did they give them strict orders not to work well?
> Both hypotheses lead to the same conclusion: the Portuguese
> did not want to supply the Congolese with technical know-

1. James Duffy, *Portuguese Africa*, p. 6, Cambridge, Mass., 1968.
2. cf. Duffy, op. cit.
3. Visconde de Paiva Manso, *História do Congo*, *Doc. I*, Lisbon, 1855.
4. See for this: Duffy, op. cit., p. 5–9.
5. Martins dos Santos, op. cit., p. 14.
6. W. G. L. Randles, *L'Ancien Royaume du Congo*, p. 103.

ledge that might be used against them and jeopardize their power.[1]

Nor was the record of the missionaries requested by the later King Afonso from Portugal any better.

> Afonso received the thirteen or fifteen priests with jubilant plans for educating and evangelizing his people, but a number of the fathers, succumbing to the moral and physical climate of the capital, found the buying and selling of slaves, in some cases with funds given them by Afonso, more lucrative.[2]

The missionaries arrived in 1508. The king had a fence set up around the place where they were to teach so that pupils could not run away. The priests left after only four days[3]. The mission itself got involved in the possession of land, the slave trade and commerce. The alliance of Portugal and the King of the Congo did not continue much longer, and the influence of Portuguese culture rapidly disappeared.

> Having to live together with other Portuguese, who had come here for purely material reasons, the missionaries were influenced by them and seduced by the temptation of riches; many of them turned to commercial activities . . . many took advantage of the first opportunity to be repatriated under pretext of the malignity of the climate—especially those who had dedicated themselves to commercial activities.[4]

It is accordingly hard to believe that, from the very beginning, the Portuguese in Africa were striving to Christianize and educate the population, that the 'expansion of the faith and of the empire' were identical, and that together with the missionaries, came the 'masters of reading and writing', and artisans 'to instruct the kin and people of the King of Congo, following his instant request'.[5]

1. Alfredo Margarido, 'L'enseignement en Afrique dite Portugaise', *Le Mois en Afrique*, August 1970, p. 63.
2. Duffy, op. cit., p. 13–14.
3. See: *Monumenta Missionaria Africana*, Vol. I, p. 30, quoted in Margarido, op. cit.
4. Martins dos Santos, op. cit., p. 17.
5. Angola (ed.), *Instituto Superior de Ciências Sociais e Política Ultramarina, Curso de Extensão Universitária Ano Lectivo de 1963–1964*, Lisbon, p. 409.

The same source indicates the real purpose of Portuguese educational policy in Africa as well as admitting its failure:

> It can, therefore, be said that the political prospects involved in our relations with the Congo, including the possibility of counting on the support by a properly-organized and relatively powerful native State, determined an educational policy which was based not only on the evangelization of the native masses but also attempted to satisfy the desire for social reorganization of the Congolese monarchs, and contribute to the expansion of Portuguese influence. This influence, however, was rapidly lost in the dynastic crises and political conflicts that followed the death of the King. The religious missions laudably insisted on remaining, but found they could give little effective religious instruction, persistently opposed by the waves of paganism from the bush. In 1624, when Mateus Cardoso, Rector of the College of Luanda, visited S. Salvador do Congo, he found no natives who could speak Portuguese, and only one who could read.[1]

Different arguments to explain why Portugal did not succeed in gaining a footing in the Congo are advanced by other authors. Eugénio Lisboa writes:

> The reasons for the failure of the experiment with the Congo are complex and probably multiple, but they are no doubt connected with the demographic upheaval caused by the slave trade, operated from São Tomé, which almost completely depopulated certain areas of the Kingdom.[2]

Basil Davidson suggests that the Portuguese attitude implied a betrayal of the Africans:

> Seldom was there a more obvious example of people asking for bread and being given a stone.[3]

There was no improvement when João III of Portugal sent out Jesuits. Two soon returned to Portugal, and the two others

1. Angola, op. cit.
2. Eugénio Lisboa, 'Education in Angola and Mozambique', in Brian Rose (ed.), *Education in Southern Africa*, p. 265, Johannesburg and London, 1970.
3. Basil Davidson, *The African Awakening*, p. 49, London, 1955.

let themselves be seduced by the temptation of riches and became traders like others who had preceded them.[1]

Of a subsequent mission of two Jesuits, one died shortly after his arrival, and the other was expelled by the King in 1555.[2]

The last vestiges gradually disappeared in the course of time. When Stanley traversed the region (1874–79), he could find no traces of Portuguese civilization or sovereignty.

In the other parts of present-day Angola (Luanda, Benguela and the surrounding territory), no Portuguese influence was perceptible until the seventeenth century. One primary school was founded by Jesuits in Luanda in 1605, the other missions occupying themselves nearly exclusively with religious teaching.[3] In 1622 formal education provided by the Jesuits was extended to include literature, theology and ethics.[4] Servants living near the school learned trades (tailoring, shoe-making, pottery, cooperage, ceramics and caulking). According to Avila de Azevedo, this was the first attempt made south of the Equator to provide occupational training.[5] However,

> It must be pointed out that, despite their missionary and educational activity, the Jesuits, in so far as their action in Angola was concerned, were frequently accused of taking part in slave trading with South America, which became so notoriously scandalous that it greatly affected the Angolan economy. The Society of Jesus even had its own ships which engaged in the slave traffic between Angola and Brazil.[6]

Such education as was provided in the colony was almost exclusively in Jesuit hands. Facilities were accordingly still further reduced when, in the middle of the eighteenth century, the Government of the Marquis of Pombal expelled the Jesuits from Portugal.

Mozambique

The Portuguese landed in Mozambique in the fifteenth century, and found it much more difficult to penetrate than Angola. Islam had

1. Martins dos Santos, op. cit., p. 21–2.
2. ibid., p. 22.
3. Angola, op. cit., p. 410.
4. Avila de Azevedo, *Política do Ensino em África*, Junta de Investigaçoes do Ultramar, p. 119, Lisbon, 1958.
5. Avila de Azevedo, 'Educaçao em Africa', *Estudos Ultramarinos* (Lisbon), No. 3, 1962, p. 109.
6. Eugénio Lisboa, op. cit., p. 267.

already taken deep roots. Moreover the newcomers faced 'the indocility of the inhabitants in the southern part'.[1] Vasco de Gama, who stopped in Mozambique on one of his voyages to India (1500), spoke of a people with a culture superior to that of the Portuguese. A local, mainly Swahili, élite lived in cities that were administered by Arabs who had passed on their culture, language and religion. Arab influence extended along the Zambezi river. The first Portuguese mission in Mozambique was established in the area of the Cuama rivers (tributaries of the Zambezi). African hostility to the Portuguese missionaries culminated in the assassination of the Jesuit D. Goncalo da Silveira when he tried, in 1560, to convert Monomotapa, ruler of Zambezia and lord of its mythical but non-existent gold mines.[2] It took another seventy years before Portuguese missionaries (in 1629) succeeded in converting Monomotapa. Zambezia then became a region strongly influenced by the Catholic Church, especially the Jesuits and the Dominicans who, however, were hostile to each other.[3]

The Dominicans lived in Vila de Sena, commercial centre of the Zambezi area. They succeeded precisely in the districts in which the Jesuits had failed, evangelizing as far as Lake Nyasa. The Jesuits, with headquarters on the Isle of Mozambique, founded an institution that, from 1610 to 1760, provided both a seminary and a hospital.[4] However, as Silva Rego states, 'the decadence increased as rapidly as the jungle grows on monsoon rains'[5]—starting at the beginning of the eighteenth century and accentuated after the Marquis de Pombal had banished the Jesuits from Portugal.

> Few governors during the century were not accused of corruption and easy financial dealings, and lesser officials made their fortunes at the expense of the government or in violation of the law. In this milieu of laxity, the conduct of the Dominicans offered hardly a refreshing contrast. 'Scandalous' is one of the milder epithets used against the Order's conduct in the eighteenth and nineteenth centuries. 'The Dominican friars [at Sena] . . . are violent and oppressive in their behaviour. . . . The promulgation of knowledge is most strenuously opposed by the priests as utterly subversive

1. Moçambique (ed.), *Instituto Superior de Ciências Sociais e Política Ultramarina, Curso de Extensão Universitária Ano Lectivo de 1965–1966*, Lisbon, p. 638.
2. Eugénio Lisboa, op. cit., p. 266.
3. Duffy, op. cit., p. 108.
4. Avila de Azevedo, *Política de Ensino em Africa*, op. cit., p. 122.
5. Quoted in Moçambique, op. cit., p. 639.

of their power, its strongest support being the ignorance of the people.' In violation of their vow of poverty, Dominicans in Zambezia held great tracts of land which they administered like any *prazero*, collecting head taxes and dealing in slaves. Some Dominicans also took over civil and administrative responsibilities. Although they accepted such charges because there were so few Portuguese men in the interior, and although they did help to maintain Portuguese sovereignity there, these activities were not always consistent with their missionary duties. To the detriment of their one-time evangelical zeal, some Jesuits also participated in agricultural and mining ventures along the river. Missionaries from other Orders, and secular priests, also acted in the spirit of the times.[1]

The West African colonies

The Cape Verde Islands had been discovered in 1444, and Guinea had been regarded, since 1446, as a district of Cape Verde. Even 200 years later there was practically no sign in either of Portuguese educational or even religious activity. The Jesuit António Vieira stopped at Cape Verde in 1652 on his way to Brazil. He asked João IV of Portugal for missionaries to teach the population of Guinea, where 'because of the lack of missionaries to evangelize and educate them, no vestiges of Christianity can be found except a few crosses in their villages and the names of the saints'.[2]

A present-day missionary wrote as follows in a book on Cape Verde published by the Institute for Overseas Studies:

> The discoveries fitted into a grandiose religious policy which viewed India as offering a means of attacking Islam from behind and as being nearer its religious and economic bases. It is thus easy to understand why, after starting with the coast of Guinea, the missionary occupation of the east coast of Africa was left aside until the fundamental purpose was achieved.[3]

This offers some insight into the strategy of Portuguese expansion, but is neither a completely correct nor an adequate explanation.

---

1. Duffy, op. cit., p. 111.
2. Joaquim Angélico de Jusus Guarra, S.J., *Ocupaçao Missionaria de Cabo Verde, Guiné, Sao Tomé e Príncipe*, p. 511, Lisbon: Instituto Superior de Ciências Sociais e Política Ultramarina, Curso de Extensao Universitária Ano Lectivo de 1965–66.
3. ibid., p. 510.

A certain interest in the Cape Verde Islands was shown from the very beginning. So low was their population density that they had first to be peopled. A mission was founded, in 1466, only twenty-two years after they were discovered. A diocese was established in Ribeira Grande in 1532, of which Praia became the seat in 1614.[1]

Henry the Navigator himself had displayed great interest in Guinea. Zurara, in his *Crônica da Guiné* tells of the

> ... great desire which [the Infante] had to increase the holy faith of Our Lord Jesus Christ, and to bring to it all the souls that might want to be saved.[2]

He immediately sent a priest, Padre Polono, to Guinea and arranged in his testament (1460) for priests to be sent to Guinea from the *Ordem de Cristo* of which he was the administrator.[3]

Portugal, here as elsewhere, pursued the policy of taking Africans to Portugal to be educated there and steeped in Portuguese culture. Jerome Münzer reports that in Lisbon he saw

> ... many negroes, who had been compelled by the King to practice the Christian religion and to learn to read and write Latin. ... A short time ago the King sent to São Tomé black priests whom he had had educated, from their child-hood, in Lisbon.[4]

There must therefore have been other reasons why the local population was denied education. The missionary quoted above gives a very detailed description of missionary activities in Cape Verde and Guinea. In Guinea there

> ... had been some [priests] who did not even say Mass, dedicating themselves more to trade than to their Religion ... the most current merchandise in those territories [were] slaves. [The priests, however, did not forget their religious duties, for] ... the missionaries then began with their instructions, sermons, hearing confessions, and charitable work, particularly among the slaves who had been brought from Guinea in great numbers. These had been baptized in

1. *Portugal Missionário*, Cucujães, 1929.
2. de Jusus Guarra, S.J., op. cit., p. 508.
3. ibid., p. 508-9.
4. ibid., p. 509.

batches of 300, 400 and 500, before being taken to Brazil or to the West Indies. For the priests saw to it that they were given a suitable education.[1]

These quotations help us to understand why, despite Portugal's interest in Cape Verde and Guinea, no effort was made to educate their populations and why António Vieira did not find any 'vestiges of Christianity' (see above). The real explanation for this interest is given by Manuel Severim de Faria (1583–1655):

> As is well known to those acquainted with the affairs of this kingdom, the contracts and rights of the coast of Guinea have for many years been the principal source of revenue of the Crown of Portugal; with this it became rich, and provided the finances to make conquests in the East and in the New Worlds.[2]

So much attention has been devoted here to educational policy in Africa during this first period because two aspects of it are particularly significant.

First, there are certain parallels (which did not exist at all periods) between later Portuguese Colonial policy and then as regards the officially proclaimed aims. Until 1974, the official thesis was that the African population was willingly assimilating Portuguese civilization; civilizing aims (and in particular religion) were put forward to disguise economic and political interests; education was never allowed to get beyond a very low minimum level, so as not to endanger acquired privileges; a very limited African élite was educated for one purpose only: to support Portuguese hegemony and act as an intermediary between the colonial machinery and the African population.

Secondly, present-day colonialism attempted to falsify Portuguese colonial history. Portuguese chroniclers (Zurara, Rui de Pina), contemporary archives and foreign sources available in modern times, all amply testify that the declared aims and methods were far from being the real ones. The aim of the falsification was twofold. Glorification of the past was designed to awaken a patriotism that had the Portuguese people themselves to regard the official colonial policy—and more especially the colonial wars—as a 'national duty'

1. de Jusus Guarra, op. cit., p. 511, 514–15.
2. ibid., p. 512–13.

and, accordingly to support it. Again, history as propagated was intended to represent colonialism as a valuable contribution to the development of mankind, and hence to justify the Portuguese colonial presence in Africa.

Educational policy under the Liberal Government

The educational work of the missions further deteriorated when the Marquis de Pombal expelled the Jesuits from all Portuguese dominions in 1759. They were not allowed back until the second half of the nineteenth century (except for a few French Jesuits who were admitted during the years 1829–34). By 1800, there were 9 or 10 fathers in Angola and perhaps 25 parish priests, half of them Angolans; while in Mozambique, in 1825, there were 10 clerics, 7 of them from Goa.[1] Thus when a Liberal Government came to power in 1834, and abolished all religious orders by decree, this did not cause any considerable change in the activities of the missions in the colonies.

The French Revolution and the Napoleonic wars hastened the end of the *ancien régime* in Portugal. A struggle between Constitutionalists and Monarchists ended in victory for the Liberals in 1834. Liberalism became more moderate under the pressure of constant opposition to it but continued in power in Portugal until the abolition of the Monarchy in 1910.

Under the Liberal Government, the State took the place of the missions in providing formal education, and teachers were either laymen or secular priests. The laity controlled educational policy. Attempts were also made to withdraw education from the control of the metropolis, e.g. the decree (1844) which was intended to allow the colonies of Cape Verde, Angola and Mozambique the right to organize studies in medicine and pharmacy. This failed, but provides undoubted evidence of a new mentality and the desire to create a new legal structure for education.[2]

The turning point was the decree (1845) establishing public schools in the colonies.

Until then, governmental interest had been limited and sporadic. Education had been left almost entirely to the missions. There were

---

1. Duffy, op cit., p. 112 and 120; also Avila de Azevedo, *Política do Ensino em Africa*, op. cit., p. 122.
2. Margarido, op. cit.

a few private initiations also. Francisco de Sousa Coutinho had started two geometry classes in Luanda; Miguel António de Melo introduced classes in arithmetic, geometry and trigonometry with a view to training accountants and topographers.[1] However, these facilities were primarily intended for the children of white officials, and were always in Luanda or Mozambique.

> In 1808, for example, the wife of Angola's Governor Saldanha de Gama gave classes in French and music to the daughters of Luanda's illustrious families.[2]

The decree of 1845 made provision for education at two levels. The first level was to be provided in elementary schools which would be established where necessary, and teach reading, writing, arithmetic, Christian doctrine, and the history of Portugal. The second level was to be provided in what were called principal schools, to be set up only in the capitals of Mozambique, Angola, São Tomé and Cape Verde, with the following curriculum: Portuguese, drawing, geometry, book-keeping, economy of the colony and applied physics.[3]

The legislation was of outstanding importance. It was unique in making no legal distinction between Africans and Europeans. This was in accordance with the liberal egalitarian principles that forbade any kind of discrimination.

Unfortunately, the euphoria did not last long. Pressure was exerted by the Portuguese settlers, and they succeeded in imposing their ideas of 'primitive peoples'. A new educational system, again based largely on the missions, was introduced by decree in 1869. It defined the different kinds of education to be given to Africans and 'Europeans' respectively. Elementary school was divided into two levels. For pupils who lived less than 3 kilometres from a school, attendance became obligatory. Special needlework schools were set up for girls. The principal schools, up to then with a higher class, were declared to be secondary schools, and tentatively introduced the teaching of foreign languages (English, French and Arabic).[4]

The Navy and Overseas Minister Rebelo da Silva, justifying the new changes, stated that, although the former system 'fulfilled an

---

1. Eugénio Lisboa, op. cit., p. 266.
2. Duffy, op. cit., p. 367–8.
3. Avila de Azevedo, *Política do Ensino em Africa*, op. cit., p. 124–5.
4. ibid., p. 125–6.

important service, . . . local difficulties, negligence and imperfect organization annulled or paralyzed its good effects.[1]

The changes did not work well in the principal schools, with the exception of the one in Luanda which, however, had a mere thirty pupils and soon ceased to exist.

In 1873, 456 boys and 33 girls attended schools in Angola. In the mid-1870s, the total attending primary schools in Mozambique was about 400.[2] No primary school was established in Lourenço Marques until 1907.[3] At the end of the century, Mousinho de Albuquerque, who detested the Liberals, commented on the educational programme as follows:

> . . . the education system was nonsense and folly. Eternally preoccupied about assimilation with the metropolis, schools were scattered along the coast; even in the interior, there were schools where improvised teachers claimed to offer primary instruction to native children. Attendance at these schools was minimal, even when they were turned over to secular priests; the profit derived, none. But, since the arrangements resembled what Portugal had, the Liberal spirit of symmetry was satisfied. The schools were a fiction.
> . . . As far as I am concerned, what we have to do to educate and civilize the *indígena* is to develop his aptitude for manual labour in a practical way and take advantage of him for the exploitation of the province.[4]

The decrees of 1845 and 1869 had not excluded the possibility of support for the work of the missionaries. In December 1868, certain advantages were offered by decree to priests who had remained in São Tomé, Angola and Mozambique. The number of missionaries in the colonies was seventy-five in 1885 and soon rose to 200 (mostly Jesuits). The increase can be explained by the international situation. The Berlin Conference (1885) and the Brussels Conference (1887) had approved

> . . . the free and public practice of all beliefs and the right to organize missions belonging to any religion, in the territories dependent on the States participating.

1. Duffy, op. cit., p. 257.
2. ibid.
3. Sampaioe Melo, *Política Indígena*, p. 119, Porto, 1910.
4. Duffy, op. cit., p. 258.

This led the Portuguese Government to support the Catholic missions in order to forestall the danger of Protestant missions filling the gap and influencing Africans,—cf. Silva Rego:

> . . . one understands the anxiety of the Government to attract many priests to the missions, in order to impede the increasing denationalizing influence of the Protestant missions.[1]

The arrival of English Baptists in northern Angola in 1878 was followed by an influx of Christian missionaries from other European countries and America. These also added to facilities for education, the facilities often following the expansion of administrative control and a more effective occupation of the interior. A certain educational pattern developed. Government and private schools were available in populated areas and centres of administration, while mission schools mostly served Africans in the rural areas. The two systems were, in principle, totally separate.

By the turn of the century, a considerable number of assimilated mulattos and Africans were concerned about the inadequacy of educational opportunity and began writing about it in local newspapers. The government discussed the issue but did practically nothing to improve the situation. Educational administration was analogous to that in Portugal, and the public schools continued to confine themselves to giving a limited number of children an opportunity of learning something of Portuguese culture and language.

Those in charge of the mission schools were primarily concerned with making converts. If Catholic, they received financial support from the government. Teaching was generally in the local African language, sometimes in Portuguese; the curriculum consisted mainly of the Catechism. However, a seminar in Angola and a technical school in Mozambique provided the first post-primary education available before the First World War. The Protestant missions frequently employed African clergy and hence usually taught in African languages. Some of the more advanced Protestant students learnt English or, sometimes, Portuguese. The use of African languages limited the level the school could reach and alienated the Portuguese, already uneasy about the presence of foreign missionaries.[2]

---

1. Angola, op. cit., p. 412.
2. The last three paragraphs are based upon D. M. Abshire and M. A. Samuels (eds.), *Portuguese Africa, A Handbook*, p. 178-9, London and New York, 1969.

School development was slow. In 1909, Mozambique had forty-eight primary schools for boys, eight for girls, and some commercial and agricultural schools. Most primary schools were run by Catholic missions. The total of mulatto and African pupils (1,195) showed no change since 1900. In Angola, where there were sixty-nine schools, the total increased by fifteen from 1900 to 1908 (1,845 to 1,860).[1]

Lay missions

Portugal was proclaimed a republic in 1910. A law passed in 1913 provided for the separation of Church and State, and replaced religious by lay missions (*missões laicas to missões civilizadoras*) which it was hoped would be more effective in Africa. The educational work of the Catholic missions, no longer financially supported by the government, practically ceased. The lay missions, working through schools and workshops, were required to supplement formal education by occupational training. Incidentally, the Governor of Mozambique, General José Machado, refused to apply this law in Mozambique.[2]

The new teachers (*agentes da civilização*) had to have completed primary school teacher training and possess some knowledge of the local languages in areas in which they were to work. Each lay mission school was to have a primary teacher who would be the director, and assistants, who would be masons, blacksmiths or farmers. Teacher training has been provided since 1917 in the Colonial Institute (*Instituto das Missões Coloniais*), the former missionary College of Cernache do Bomjardim, founded by the Jesuits in 1855. Candidates for the five-year basic course had to have completed secondary school, and also follow a special course dealing with the specific problems of the colonies. Subjects included agriculture, hygienics, geodesy, and the basic principles of law and educational theory.

The curriculum proved too ambitious. With much too few teachers reaching its standards set, the lay missions were probably doomed to failure from the start. There were admittedly some successes, but most of the lay missions could not meet the standards demanded.[3] The result was a new decree in 1919, again allowing the Catholic missions financial support from the State. It recognized the Catholic missions

---

1. Sampaio e Melo, op. cit., p. 119–20.
2. Moçambique, op. cit., p. 641.
3. M. Borges Grainha, *As missões em Angola e Moçambique*, p. 14, Cernache do Bomjardim, 1920.

only as 'elements of civilizing activity', but this cannot disguise the defeat of the lay mission idea, officially confirmed seven years later (1926), when the Colonial Minister of the 'National Dictatorship' (i.e. the Salazar régime), abolished the lay missions by decree (No. 12336). A chapter of this decree deals with education, including the conditions of agricultural and occupational apprenticeship.

There were fierce controversies during the 1920s regarding the merits of individual *v.* mass, and academic *v.* technical education. Because of their significance here, the principal arguments put forward in a discussion between two of the main protagonists (the colonial High Commissioner Norton de Matos, who advocated the lay missions, and Vicente Ferreira) are worth reproducing. Norton de Matos, referring to the educational work done in the colony of Angola, stated:

> The population of Angola has the following five elements. In the last place, there are the great mass of the inhabitants of the Province, still in the darkness of the primitive civilizations. Next a limited number of natives who by a most unsuitable form of instruction have been given some rudiments of reading and writing without any care to the shaping of their characters, so creating a factor harmful and detrimental to the future society. There are, then, a fortunately ever-decreasing number of Europeans who, for various and always lamentable reasons, integrate themselves into native life and civilization and can only with difficulty be prised away from both. Pride of place goes to the growing numbers of natives who, through unceasing efforts and their determination to rid themselves of the darkness of the past, have overcome their own mistaken opposition: despite the almost total lack of schools, they act like civilized people, worthy of all our consideration. Finally, there are the increasingly numerous European families, the merchants, farmers, manufacturers and public servants to whom our country owes so much for the grandiose work they have accomplished during the last twenty years, with the greatest tenacity and perseverance, and also with the greatest patriotism.[1]

Warning of the 'risks' involved in allowing the native population rapid

---

1. Quoted in Angola, op. cit., p. 414–15.

access to elementary education of the metropolitan type, Norton de Matos advocates schools instead that would be more workshop than school. They would teach the Portuguese language, writing and reading, and a knowledge of arithmetic, weights and measurements and then—according to the place and local customs—trade, agriculture, or working with wood, stone or metal.

It was to the basic workshop principle of educating through working that Vicente Ferreira objected:

> The most tangible and evident result of the famous education through work principle as practiced in the school-workshops is the formation of an indigenous proletariat that is easier for capitalists to exploit than its competitor, the European proletariat, with the aggravating factor that feelings of revolt are intensified by inevitable racial hatred. The school will not achieve its social purpose; it will, up to a certain point, be effective only in training men to be working machines.

To avoid such evils which, in his view, would lead to the break-up of communities, he advocated collective rather than individual education, and what later came to be known as community development. The schoolmaster, the doctor, those who trained people in agriculture and in working the main local materials and the administrative authorities, should be the active agents in providing this education.

Norton de Matos and Vicente Ferreira were both against a purely academic education, seeing in it a source of conflicts that would be hard to control.

A significant point in educational policy was reached in a decree adopted in 1921 which forbade the use of African languages in schools, except for the purpose of teaching religion and in the early stages of teaching the Portuguese language. The government felt that, since the purpose of education was African integration into Portuguese society and culture, the use of African languages was senseless and divisive. Most Africans lived, of course, far from centres where there was any need to speak Portuguese, so that there was neither any demand nor much possibility of practising what was for most Africans a foreign language. One result of the decree was to give a natural advantage to Catholic missions—compounded by Protestant intransigence or linguistic inadequacy in Portuguese.[1]

1. Duffy, op. cit., p. 179–80.

The government tried very hard to harness the foreign missions to Portuguese interests—not only the Protestant missions, which were allowed to teach only under permanent State control,[1] but also the foreign Catholic missions. The compulsory use of Portuguese in teaching provided a good way of forestalling attempts by other colonial powers to annex the colonies. Norton de Matos makes this clear:

> The establishment of lay and religious missions is of the greatest importance and will contribute much to civilization in Angola and to the improvement of the material and moral conditions of the life of its indiginous inhabitants, on the following conditions:
> (a) that Portuguese missions are more numerous and efficient than the foreign missions;
> (b) that teaching is exclusively in Portuguese;
> (c) that both sexes are taught suitable subjects and occupations, to the almost total exclusion of academic subjects.[2]

The new policy was not likely to raise the level of education, which continued to remain inferior even to that of other colonies:

> The reports of the African Education Commission—which surveyed African education under the auspices of the Phelps-Stokes Fund and the foreign mission societies of North America and Europe and visited Angola in 1921 and Mozambique in 1924—gave a generally dismal picture of conditions in the provinces. The Commission noted the hostility to Protestant missions, the practice of excluding native languages from the schools, misunderstanding and apathy in provincial government circles, lack of funds, and no encouragement of African teachers. Not only was the present state of education in Angola and Mozambique backward, especially in comparison with other colonial areas, but observations in Portuguese Africa . . . offer practically no basis for hope of any essential improvements in colonial policy.[3]

The *Estado Novo*

The military putsch of 28 May 1926 that set up the National Dictator-

---

1. John T. Tucker, *Angola. Land of the Blacksmith Prince*, p. 111–13, London, 1933.
2. Norton de Matos, 'A Província de Angola', in Margarido, op. cit., p. 74.
3. cf. Duffy, op. cit., p. 259.

ship considerably strengthened the position of the Catholic Church, since it was a Catholic party that came to power. One result was the decree of December 1926 (already mentioned) abolishing the lay missions. Three months earlier, the Statute of the Catholic Missions— which the Institute for Overseas Studies referred to as 'honestly marking a new and patriotic policy'[1]—entrusted education in Angola to the Catholic missions: after the Liberal Government interlude in the nineteenth century and the brief period from 1911 to 1919 when the State refused to give financial support to the Catholic missions, the Church's christianizing, educational, nationalizing and civilizing role was once again officially recognized. Article 140 of the Constitution of 1933 stated that:

> The Portuguese Catholic missions overseas and the establishments for training personnel for their services . . . shall be protected and assisted by the State, as being institutions of education and assistance and instruments of civilization.

The Catholic missions regained their former influence after the prohibition of the lay missions in 1926. The Colonial Act (1930) defined the purpose of education for the 'indigenous population' as being to lead them from their 'primitive' to a civilized condition, so that the *indígena* would become Portuguese and work and be 'useful to society', within the context set out in Article 2:

> It belongs to the organic character of the Portuguese Nation to fulfil its historical mission: to possess and colonize overseas territories and to civilize the indigenous population living in them, thus at the same time exerting the moral influence to which it is committed by the *Padroado* over the Orient.

The schools started in Angola and Mozambique were mainly intended to serve a systematic and rationalized exploitation of the resources of the colonies. In Angola, in 1937, rural school teaching was linked to farms (*granjas administrativas*) so that a child learned reading and farming together. Later, elementary agricultural schools were set up in agricultural stations in areas due for intensive cultivation (on the same lines as Amboim, the main coffee-producing area). The agricul-

---

1. de Jusus Guarra, S.J., op. cit., p. 539.

tural school (*escola agropecuária*) of Tchinvinguiro, established for the same reasons was, for many years, the most important in Angola.[1]

Education in the normal sense of the word thus was subordinated to the objective of obtaining skilled workers without running the risk of producing thinking and critical people.

With the Missionary Statute (1941), the *Estado Novo* established a structure which was to have devastating effects on education in the colonies. Because of its significance, it will be dealt with separately here.

1. Margarido, op. cit.

2 The Missionary Statute of 1941

The Catholic missions had enjoyed a privileged position in the colonies since the accession to power of the national dictatorship in 1926. This was consolidated and institutionalized in the concordat with the Vatican signed in 1940; the annexed missionary accord was incorporated in the Missionary Statute (1941).

It is worth mentioning that, in all the negotiations involved, not a single African took part. The preliminary talks were almost exclusively between the prime minister Dr Salazar and the Patriarch of Lisbon, Cardinal Cerejeira.[1]

The privileges of the Catholic missions, dealt with only very generally in the Colonial Act of 1930, were made specific in the Missionary Statute, cf. Article 66:

> ... Education specially intended for natives shall be entirely entrusted to missionary personnel and their auxiliaries.

Separate education for Africans and Europeans, already established in practice, became more clearly defined. The educational system for Europeans and assimilated Africans was the same as in metropolitan Portugal. The great mass of the Africans had only the mission schools which provided the rudimentary education (*ensino rudimentar*) that in 1956 became functional education (*ensino de adaptação*). The three-year primary course taught Portuguese language and culture. Although there was no legal provision to prevent African pupils from subsequently attending State schools, artificial age barriers and

1. *Der totalitäre Gottesstaat*, p. 172, edited by Michael Raske *et al.* on behalf of the Arbeitsgemeinschaft von Priestergruppen in der BRD, Düsseldorf, 1970; and Ludwig Renard, 'Salazar', *Kirche und Staat in Portugal*, p. 68, Essen, 1968.

natural rural obstacles were such as to keep such transfers minimal.[1]

Avila de Azevedo points out that official rudimentary and functional education for Africans are: (a) strictly delimited in subject matter; (b) entirely in the hands of the Catholic missions; (c) limited, so far as the role of the State is concerned, to establishing programmes and curricula, and awarding examination certificates.[2] Cf. Article 68 of the Missionary Statute:

> The education of the native population shall be subject to the principles laid down in the Constitution; it shall for all purposes be considered official, and shall be regulated by the plans and programmes adopted by the governments of the colonies.

Educational control had a twofold purpose: first, to direct education in such a way that Africans become 'true Portuguese' and so accepted Portuguese rule; secondly, to use education to produce good agricultural workers and craftsmen who would usefully serve the colonial economy. Cf. the continuation of Article 68:

> The aim of these plans and programmes shall be to make the native population national and moral, and to inculcate such work habits and skills for each sex as suit the conditions and requirements of the regional economics; moral education shall aim at curing laziness and preparing future rural workers and craftsmen to produce what they need to satisfy their own requirements and their social obligations.
>
> The education of the indigenous population shall thus be essentially nationalist and practical, the native then being able to gain a living for himself and his family; and it shall take due account of the social condition and psychology of the populations for whom it is intended. . . .

The former Overseas Minister Silva Cunha confirmed in the midfifties that these principles were still upheld:

> . . . By this means we are attempting to accelerate the assimilation or complete 'Portuguezation' of the natives,

---

1. See Duffy, op. cit., p. 180.
2. Avila de Azevedo, *Política de Ensimo em África*, op. cit., p. 131.

and to help improve their material situation by training them for more economically valid activities.[1]

Article 69 states:

> In the schools, the teaching and use of the Portuguese language shall be obligatory. Outside school, the missionaries and the assistants shall also use the Portuguese language. In religious education, however, the indigenous language may freely be used.

Article 17 empowered the government to reject missionaries who could not read and write Portuguese properly, independently of whether or not they knew African languages. The fact that the missions could teach religion in the indigenous languages but had to transact everything else in Portuguese could hardly do much to strengthen religious instruction, since it divorced it from everyday life. On the other hand Church leaders have usually regarded education not as something in its own right but as a means of furthering religion. This explains at least in part why, despite State subsidies, the educational activities of the missions have had such limited effect.[2]

To ensure 'Portuguezation', the Missionary Statute stipulated that all bishops, apostolic vicars and prefects to whom Catholic missionaries are subject must be of Portuguese nationality, and that all missionary school staff employed in training African teachers must be Portuguese.

The procedure for the nomination of bishops was the same in the colonies as in the metropolis. The government could veto any candidate who was politically inacceptable to it. The right had to be exercised within thirty days. All relevant negotiations were secret (Article 7).

The Church was not only used to help the State in implementing its colonial policy, but served to provide the State with an argument to legitimize its presence in Africa. The former Overseas Minister Silva Cunha, speaking in Luanda in 1964 said:[3]

> With the help of God and our own determination, we saved the foundation of our rights. . . . We continued to civilize

1. Silva Cunha, *Administraçao e Direito Colonial*, Vol. I, p. 161, Lisbon, Ediçao da Associaçao Académica da Faculdade de Direito, 1957.
2. See Margarido, op. cit.
3. Joaquim M. da Silva Cunha, *Portuguese Angola*, Lisbon, 1964, quoted in: Renard, op. cit., p. 88.

and to convert the land to Christianity. . . . Even if we believed that Portugal set out to expand from purely economic motives, it has been the most ardent and effective paladin of Christianity in the modern world.

He spoke of Portugal's

mission of bringing pagan and infidel peoples to the light of the Christian faith. . . . Through it, in all continents, many peoples have become Christian and Portuguese, so that now the national community is geographically dispersed and racially multiform, but nontheless deeply united.

He ended with a reference to the many soldiers, missionaries, scientists and farmers

who made this the land it now is, thoroughly Portuguese, with all the defects and virtues of the Portuguese; who made it what it is so that it could continue . . . and remain Portuguese, totally Portuguese, only Portuguese.

This could not be said to be against the desire and interests of the Catholic Church, which has supported the *Estado Novo* since its installation in 1926. Its chief spokesman, the Patriarch of Lisbon, Cardinal Cerejeira, was unequivocal:[1]

Portugal has been the pioneer of Christian civilization throughout the world. It is to Portugal that the peoples are looking with hope. One may already ask if Portugal is not again bringing light to the world.

In his contribution to a post-graduate course given in 1965–66 in the Institute for Overseas Studies of the Technical University of Lisbon, the Jesuit missionary Joaquim Guarra explained why the Catholic Church acted as an extension of the Portuguese colonial State. Referring to the privileged position which the Catholic missions had regained in the *Estado Novo*, he states:[2]

The miracle was worked by our Lady of Fatima, to whom

1. Quoted in : *Der totalitäre Gottesstant*, op. cit., p. 175.
2. Joaquim Angélico de Jusus Guarra, S.J., op. cit., p. 540–1. Lúcia is one of the three children of the village of Fatima who, in 1917, reported seeing visions of the Virgin Mary (Our Lady of Fatima). Lúcia subsequently entered a religious order.

our country belongs. So I said one day, when Sister Lúcia, who was present, observed: 'Yes, but through Prof. Oliveira Salazar'. With his collaborators, I would add. The *Estado Novo* is an awakening of the national conscience to the mission which God assigned to us, is Providence giving us for this purpose capacities and resources which we must exploit.

It was precisely this attitude of the Catholic Church in Portugal that led the State to support it, to entrust it with the education of the African populations in the colonies, and to grant it 'entirely unrestrained development' (Article 15 of the Missionary Accord).

The Catholic missions received financial support from the governments of Portugal and of the colony concerned (Article 43, and Article 9 of the Missionary Accord), as well as land (sites in Angola and Mozambique of up to 2,000 hectares) (Article 52). Under the Accord they were exempt from property tax (Article 11); resident bishops, vicars and apostolic prefects were guaranteed an appropriate honorarium and a pension (Article 12); travel expenses were reimbursed within and outside the colonies (Article 14).

Thanks to this privileged position, the missions were able to expand. In Mozambique, numbers increased from forty-four missioners in 1940 to 147 in 1960, and the numbers of African pupils receiving rudimentary or functional instruction from 95,444 in 1942–43 to 385,259 in 1960–61.[1] However, apart from the attendance figures, the results were frankly disappointing; cf. The Institute for Overseas Studies:[2]

> . . . No tables of functional education results was prepared. The official statistics are, in general, quite incomplete and any table drawn from them would be misleading. In any case, these figures, although partial, leave no margin for doubt as to the low level of progress.

The results of Portuguese educational policy in the colonies are eloquently illustrated by the illiteracy rates revealed in the 1950 census (see Table 2).

Taking the African population alone, the illiteracy rate was still

1. Moçambique, op. cit., p. 645.
2. ibid., p. 659.

TABLE 2. Illiteracy

	Total population	Illiterate population	Percentage of illiterates
Angola	4,145,266	4,019,834	96.97
Cape Verde	148,331	116,844	78.50
Guinea	510,777	504,928	98.85
Mozambique	5,738,911	5,615,053	97.86

Sources: Anuário Estatístico do Ultramar 1958, Instituto Nacional de Estatística, Lisbon, and calculations by the author.

higher, since the same sources indicate a considerably lower rate among whites.

Estimated literacy rates for the entire population: Mozambique (1955), 4-6 per cent; Angola (1966), 12-13 per cent. In Angola it was estimated that 60 per cent of the Europeans were literate and 10 per cent of Africans.[1]

Eugéno Lisboa comments as follows on rudimentary and functional education:[2]

> ... The low level of this education, because of the shortage of qualified teachers and monitors, also fostered the conviction that it was second class education, for natives only; the very small salaries paid to the teachers and monitors no doubt further strengthened this impression. The per capita cost was very much lower than that of the government primary schools. Hence the missions—made responsible for functional education—are somewhat unfairly blamed, as the means at their disposal were in no way commensurate with their task. This, of course, does not excuse the often serious errors made by those who administered this type of education in mission schools. . . . Another major criticism is that, although to a certain extent it is a kind of preparatory education for normal primary education, the African pupil had no access to government schools unless he had citizenship as an 'assimilated' African; and citizenship was not acquired by attending school, but through a long administrative process. The same is even more true of secondary education, mainly provided in government schools. The statistics indicate that the number of assimilated Africans,

1. Allison Butler Herrick *et al.*, *Area Handbook for Mozambique*, p. 93, Washington, 1969; Allison Butler Herrick *et al.*, *Area Handbook for Angola*, p. 122, Washington, 1967.
2. Eugénio Lisboa, op. cit., p. 277.

both in Angola and in Mozambique, was always insignificant, which further accounts for the discriminatory nature of this type of education.

It can thus be said that education for Africans in the Portuguese colonies—including that provided under the terms of the Missionary Accord—was not only discriminatory, but largely inefficient. It is Africans who suffer the consequences. But, as we shall see later, the Catholic Church itself is, in the long run, the victim of the educational system it advocated and supported, i.e. of its ambition to have a monopoly of the education of Africans. The Portuguese State, on the other hand, achieved two objectives: it reduced expenditure for the colonial budget—one of the major concerns of Salazar—because mission education cost the State much less than would a government educational system; secondly, since the missions took responsibility for the education and its results, they and not the State, would be criticized for its shortcomings.

It is evident that, even if they wanted to, the missions were not in a position to live up to this task and responsibility.[1] This affords them no escape from the criticisms—particularly at the lack of teacher qualification—voiced in later years, when the shortcomings had become so evident and enormous that they could no longer be passed over in silence despite the Church's efforts to hush allegations of its own incapacity.

Professor Silva Rego, expert on missionary questions in the Institute for Overseas Studies, commented as follows in 1964:[2]

> . . . Without economic resources, how could the Church face the obligation it had previously so cheerfully and gladly accepted? It could do little more than what it had already been doing for some time. . . . The Church's calumniators have not let the opportunity slip of trying to sabotage the measures advocated by the Missionary Accord and implemented in the Missionary Statute. Anticlericalism has throughly exploited the partial but undisputed failure of the Church, economically helpless before the enormous task it had undertaken to carry through successfully. There are those who said: Is this, then, all the Church can do?

1. The following remarks are based upon Margarido, op. cit.
2. António da Silva Rego, 'Consideraçoes sobre o ensino missionário', *Ultramar 1964*, p. 15–27, quoted in: Margarido, op. cit., p. 78.

Would it not be more sensible to return to official education, exclusively official education, and reduce missionary education to a purely auxiliary role? In the end, the Church succeeded in teaching the Catechism, and hardly anything more. . . .

The sorry condition of educational affairs by the end of the 1950s forced the government, under the pressure of internal and external factors which will now be examined, to attempt more and to devise a form of education less narrow than that provided for Africans by the missions under the Missionary Statute.

3 Education and science under colonialism until 1974

The reforms of the 1960s

A general survey of the present state of education and science in the colonies would be outside the scope of this study and would complicate its specific purpose of assessing the effects of Portuguese colonialism on the colonies. The reader is accordingly referred to other sources.[1]

Political and economic changes in Western Europe after the Second World War; the development of capitalism in Portugal itself; and the pressure exerted by liberation movements compelled Portugal to take a new course in her colonial policy. This involved accelerated economic development (mainly by training the labour force) in the colonies, and a more forceful policy of assimilation.

As an integral part of the colonial policy in general, educational policy underwent fundamental changes. Education was an evident weak point, subject in itself to considerable criticism; this weakness, moreover, was preventing the proper use of manpower now necessary for development, research and the application of new techniques.

Table 3 shows the state of education in the colonies at the beginning of 1960.

Although statistical comparisons must be treated with caution, it can safely be said that the school enrolment ratios (Table 4) were considerably lower in 1960 than those of neighbouring countries. A more advanced economy in the colonies would be possible only if it were feasible to draw on both Europeans and on skilled Africans. This implied generalizing and Africanizing lay education instead of depending only on education by the missions.

1. See for example, Eugénio Lisboa, op. cit.; Herrick *et al.*, *Area Handbook for Angola*, op. cit.; Herrick *et al.*, *Area Handbook for Mozambique;* op. cit.; Duffy, op. cit.

The basis for this new kind of education was created by the abolition of the *estatuto indígena* immediately after the beginning of the armed revolt in Angola in 1961. This is regretted by Silva Rego:[1]

> The abolition of the *estatuto indígena* a few years ago provided the legal foundation for not complying with the terms of the Missionary Statute of 1941, viz. 'Education specially intended for the native population shall be entirely entrusted to missionary personnal and their auxiliaries'. And when the Government recently decided to reform primary education overseas, there was no lack of desire to demand greater secularization, a greater degree of official intervention, and a greater divorce from missionary activity.

A thorough reform of primary education, already in force since 1961, was made official by Decree No. 45908 in September 1964. The distinction between indigenous and non-indigenous was abolished, and the institutions set up in accordance with it were appropriately adapted. In education, this meant in practice the abolition of a type of education specially intended for Africans.

Primary education was made compulsory for all children between 6 and 12 years of age, on the same lines as in metropolitan Portugal except for the stipulation made in Article 1 of the decree that it be adapted to local conditions.

In 1967, attendance at the fifth and sixth years of primary school was made compulsory in Portugal for all children who had completed the fourth primary class and did not intend to go on to secondary school. This provision was also extended to the colonies but, pending the establishment of adequate facilities, was to become effective only in 1972–73.[2]

The reform deprived the missions of their specific attributions in colonial education. Their schools were not abolished, but lost their privileged position. This was the outcome of a struggle that had lasted many years. The careful formulation of the preamble to the decree gave due regard to various susceptibilities:

> ... The cooperation of the Portuguese Catholic missions with the State shall be recognized in the State's taking over of responsibility for the primary elementary education provided by them, in participation in the training of teachers, and in

1. da Silva Rego, op. cit., p. 15–27, quoted in: Margarido, op. cit., p. 79–80.
2. United Nations document A/8023/Add.3, 5 October 1970.

TABLE 3. Portuguese colonies: state of education as at 31 December 1959

Type of school	Cape Verde			Guinea		
Functional (de adaptação)						
Official (in government schools)	—	—	—	—	—	—
Catholic missions	—	—	—	160	155	10,009
Primary						
Official	125	185	7,729	13	32	1,061
Catholic missions	45	47	3,388	34	41	2,464
Vocational						
Total	5	27	777	18	34	606
Including Catholic missions	1	4	222	17	15	445
Teacher training						
Total	—	—	—	—	—	—
Secondary						
Total	2	30	1,031	1	16	249
Non-government and not subsidized by the State						
Total	5	5	182			
TOTAL	182	294	13,107	226	278	14,389

1. Figures at end of 1958.
Source: Overseas Ministry, Lisbon.

the generalization of what has already been provided for in law in Angola, namely, the allocation where necessary of State teachers to the schools of these missions.

This act of depriving the missions of their power evoked a series of strong reactions. For example, the Church in Mozambique protested to the Legislative Council that[1]

> ... the State, by removing from the Catholic missions the monopoly of functional education and taking itself the place

1. Quoted in Virgílio de Lemos, 'Evolution Politique de l'Enseignement au Mozambique', *Présence Africaine*, No. 4, 1967, p. 124.

São Tomé and Príncipe			Angola			Mozambique		
—	—	—	—	—	—	5	5	313
—	—	—	1,184	1,479	65,652	2,793	3,111	361,966
10	42	1,759	229	513	17,167	146	519	15,486
7	14	1,061	325	543	10,324	148	293	9,986
1	5	93	178	434	7,782	79	402	9,406
1	5	93	160[1]	193[1]	4,192[1]	69	167	4,918
—	—	—	2	13	325	6	26	574
1	9	171	5	132	3,523	12	161	3,129
2	4	277	510	1,094	33,653	69	297	9,075
21	74	3,361	2,433	4,118	138,426	3,258	4,814	409,935

of the Church in this work, is lessening the prestige of the missions within the schools and among the African populations; this may represent a blow to national unity and the integrity of the Fatherland.

This quotation shows how far the Catholic Church still continued—even after the liberation movements began to express clearly the protest of the colonial peoples against Portuguese domination—to regard itself as an instrument of the Portuguese colonialist State. Although assimilation continued to be the goal, and the Portuguese language, as an element of integration, remained compulsory in the

TABLE 4. School enrolment ratios 1960 (non-adjusted)[1]

Country	Primary	Secondary
Angola	9	3
Mozambique	26	2
Basutoland	78[2]	5
Congo (Brazzaville)	58	7
Congo (Leopoldville)	43	3
Kenya	49	4[3]
Cape Verde Islands	19[4]	8
Portuguese Guinea	13[5]	2
São Tomé and Príncipe	20	5
Cameroon	51	4
Ghana	40	3
Ivory Coast	31	4
Senegal	20	5

1. The unadjusted primary school enrolment ratio is the percentage ratio of enrolment in relation to the estimated population 5–14 years old; the corresponding secondary ratio is the ratio of enrolment in all types of schools (general, vocational and teacher training) at this level in relation to the estimated population 15–19 years old.
2. Africans only.
3. Including higher teacher training.
4. Not including mission schools.
5. Including Koranic schools.

Source: Unesco Statistical Yearbook, 1963.

schools, the reform paved the way for the generalization of primary education in the colonies. The new policy was not limited to primary education. The expansion of secondary education attempted to answer criticisms of earlier Portuguese educational policy. However, the stress was on technical school expansion, to meet new demands for skilled manpower. More places were provided in technical schools, and lower fees made them more attractive than ordinary schools to students from lower socio-economic levels.

Particular attention was paid to agricultural education, which was offered at secondary level in Angola and Mozambique, though not in Guinea. Elementary agricultural instruction was an essential part of the curriculum in rural schools.

Guinea did not enjoy a similar degree of expansion, but the

Governor announced in January 1973 that 'the expansion of secondary and technical education is already in preparation'.[1]

A limiting factor was the lack of teachers. Priority was accordingly given in the sixties to increasing the number of primary and secondary teacher training institutions. The training offered was free. The curriculum for primary school teacher training was the same as in Portugal except for two additional courses: *formação portugueso* (Portuguese values, past and present) and 'social activities'.

A decree (No. 44,530) promulgated in August 1963 in both Angola and Mozambique established *estados gerais* (general studies). Only the general part of these university-level studies could be taken in the colonies: the course had to be completed in Portugal. In Angola, the *estudos gerais* were decentralized, and could be taken in faculties in Luanda, Sá da Bandeira, and Nova Lisboa. In Mozambique, they were concentrated in Lourenço Marques. Under Decree No. 48,790, these faculties were given the name of universities in 1968, and authorized to award degrees.

The emphasis in the curricula of the universities was also on vocational and technical studies. In 1970, an economics faculty was added to the universities in Angola and Mozambique—an addition long advocated by private industry. Guinea has no university (as indicated above), but detailed discussions on the subject were being held with the metropolitan government at the time of writing.[2]

Changes brought about by the reforms

Portugal's new educational policy (since the beginning of the sixties) led to an improvement and expansion of education at all levels, particularly in the larger and economically more important colonies of Angola and Mozambique.

A comparison of Tables 3 and 5 makes this expansion obvious. Tables 6, 7, 8 and 9 show this development for the two extremes: Angola with the most comprehensive expansion, Guinea with the least.

It must be emphasized here that the validity of such comparisons is only relative. The educational system changed at all levels during the sixties. Moreover, the figures vary from one set of statistics to the

1. *A Capital*, 19 January 1973.
2. ibid.

next, even when published by official agencies, often because the coverage is different. It is only since 1966–67 that statistics have been officially prepared on a uniform basis. It can nevertheless be confidently stated that an expansion of education has taken place since the beginning of the sixties which is unprecedented in the Portuguese colonies.

However, the increase is merely quantitative, very often consisting of an increase in the physical numbers of schools, students and teaching staff. The lower starting point, and, as we have seen, the level of education at the beginning of the sixties was extraordinarily low. Two checks need to be applied. First, how many of the population were in fact affected? Secondly, at what level was the education which was provided? In other words, has the reform benefited Africans, and to what extent? This has become difficult to ascertain because since the abolition of the *estatuto indígena* in 1961, the official statistics (except for Mozambique), no longer distinguish between races.

A critical examination of the new educational policy of the sixties

The basic aim of the new policy was unchanged from the old, i.e. inculcating Portuguese values, and developing in pupils a conscious identification with Portugal in order to strengthen national unity. This was recommended in 1966 by the Coordinating Council for Education in the Colonies.[1] In 1970, the Provincial Secretary for Education in Angola, Pinheiro da Silva, stated that 'all education aims at the integration of the African Portuguese into the moral, spiritual and material way of life of the European Portuguese'.[2] The Rector of the University of Lourenço Marques confirmed that 'the university must be the principal vehicle for disseminating and consolidating overseas all those values that define and characterize Lusiade culture'.[3]

As the person mainly responsible for education in the colonies, the former Overseas Minister Silva Cunha stated in mid-1972:[4]

Education must therefore be eminently pragmatic in this

Continued page 85

1. *Diário de Notícias*, 6 September 1966.
2. *Notícias e Factos* (New York), ed. Casa de Portugal, No. 149, 14 August 1970.
3. *Notícias* (Lourenço Marques), 6 January 1972.
4. *Diário de Notícias*, 6 August 1972.

TABLE 5. State of education in the Portuguese colonies (1969/70)

Type of school	Cape Verde	Guinea	São Tomé and Príncipe	Angola	Mozambique[1]
Students					
Infant teaching	—	...	209	2,484	964
Primary	40,685	26,401	9,089	384,884	496,381
Secondary:					
Preparatory	2,006	1,254	901	25,137	7,307
Secondary	799	394	264	10,779	10,524
Technical occupational	302	415	113	14,660	...
Arts	—	—	—	304	...
Ecclesiastical	69	27	—	720	600
Higher education[2]	—	—	—	1,757	1,145
Teacher training	104	...	43	1,402	1,124
Teachers					
Infant teaching	—	...	5	70	29
Primary	840	463	299	8,714	6,607
Secondary:					
Preparatory	63	52	29	1,206	455
Secondary	106	22	19	936	695
Technical occupational	23	48	25	1,171	...
Arts	—	—	—	12	...
Ecclesiastical	7	5	—	66	38
Higher education[2]	—	—	—	213	213
Teacher training	11	...	11	126	120
Schools					
Infant teaching	—	...	2	43	11
Primary	332	242	45	4,000	4,095
Secondary:					
Preparatory	5	1	1	99	46
Secondary	7	1	1	61	45
Technical occupational	2	3	2	65	...
Arts	—	—	—	1	...
Ecclesiastical	1	1	—	6	6
Higher education[2]	—	—	—	5	9
Teacher training	1	2	1	15	12

1. Figures for 1968/69.
2. Including university education, ecclesiastical and social service schools.
Source: Anuário Estatístico Províncias Ultramarinas 1970, Vol. II; Lisbon, Instituto Nacional de Estatística.

TABLE 6. Angola. Development of educational system, according to category, 1960–70: number of students

Type of school	1960/61	1961/62	1962/63	1963/64	1964/65	1965/66	1966/67	1967/68	1968/19	1969/70
Infant teaching	432	563	583	1,030	1,417	1,615	1,560	1,738	2,071	2,484
Primary[1]	105,781	112,326	123,641	153,088	203,377	222,326	267,768	203,099	339,681	392,809
Preparatory course to secondary education	—	—	—	—	—	—	—	—	12,903	25,137
Secondary	7,486	8,417	9,700	11,447	12,560	14,632	16,700	20,793	16,745	11,321
Technical and occupational	4,501	6,626	7,912	9,787	11,069	13,456	15,371	17,625	13,871	10,946
Elementary technical schools (commercial and industrial)	4,501	5,979	7,807	9,549	10,686	12,961	14,783	16,835	12,958	9,679
Commercial and industrial institutes	—	47	105	238	383	495	588	790	913	1,267
Agricultural schools	—	144	147	192	207	178	188	241	301	377
Elementary schools for arts and crafts	—	410	337	625	498	709	1,035	955	882	1,393
Ecclesiastical schools (secondary and high)	610	663	573	579	687	676	712	714	831	841
University	—	—	—	286	418	477	607	827	1,074	1,570
Teacher training (university level)	—	—	—	—	—	—	—	—	—	27
Teacher training	294	188	345	566	760	936	997	1,083	1,147	1,402
Schools of qualification for station school teacher	294	183	322	470	550	705	794	911	953	1,177
Primary teachers' schools	—	—	23	96	210	231	203	172	194	225
Art academy	130	101	175	163	258	147	227	598	253	304
Other[2]	—	228	56	90	259	519	594	563	5,326	4,204
TOTAL	119,234	129,066	143,469	177,853	231,510	255,671	305,759	347,236	395,094	452,815

1. Including functional.
2. Others are: social service (secondary, intermediate, high), courses for monitors, courses for nurses, training of teachers for the preparatory course to secondary education, religion, training of civil servants, training outside the official programme.

Source: *Amnário Estatístico, Angola, 1970;* Direcção Provincial dos Serviços de Estatística, Angola.

TABLE 7. Angola. Development of educational system, according to category, 1960–70: number of teachers

Type of school	1960/61	1961/62	1962/63	1963/64	1964/65	1965/66	1966/67	1967/68	1968/69	1969/70
Infant teaching	20	24	38	38	51	48	71	58	65	70
Primary[1]	2,890	3,143	3,356	3,806	4,549	4,922	5,986	6,767	7,680	8,961
Preparatory course to second education	—	—	—	—	—	—	—	—	742	1,206
Secondary	382	427	476	556	591	659	720	863	919	936
Technical and vocational	307	364	506	606	638	735	805	948	1,075	826
Elementary technical schools (commercial and industrial)	307	353	485	547	586	661	729	867	984	717
Commercial and industrial institutes	—	11	21	59	52	74	76	81	91	109
Agricultural schools	—	14	13	18	10	11	18	21	26	44
Elementary schools for arts and crafts	—	19	22	41	21	33	53	51	61	69
Ecclesiastical schools (secondary and high)	95	77	66	76	67	65	63	84	98	101
University	—	—	—	38	38	38	77	84	123	160
Teacher training (university level)	—	—	—	—	—	—	—	—	—	7
Teacher training	13	14	31	66	63	77	78	100	128	126
Schools of qualification for station school teachers	13	14	23	38	39	47	50	63	68	69
Primary teachers' schools	—	—	8	28	24	30	28	37	40	40
Art academy	7	7	11	11	9	9	11	14	13	12
Other[2]	—	63	27	48	92	111	122	158	531	496
TOTAL	3,714	4,152	4,546	5,304	6,129	6,708	8,004	9,148	11,441	13,014

1. Including functional.
2. Others are: social service (secondary, intermediate, high), courses for monitors, courses for nurses, training of teachers for the preparatory course to secondary education, religion, training of civil servants, training outside the official programme.
Source: *Anuário Estatístico*, Angola, 1970; Direcçao Provincial dos Serviços de Estatística, Angola.

TABLE 8. Angola. Development of educational system, according to category, 1960–70: number of schools

Type of school	1960/61	1961/62	1962/63	1963/64	1964/65	1965/66	1966/67	1967/68	1968/69	1969/70
Infant teaching	8	8	11	16	21	22	22	32	36	43
Primary[1]	2,011	2,031	2,329	2,360	2,561	2,660	3,237	3,489	3,803	4,211
Preparatory course to secondary education	—	—	—	—	—	—	—	—	83	99
Secondary	40	44	46	45	52	55	54	58	66	61
Technical and occupational	17	23	28	33	36	40	38	51	59	45
Elementary technical schools (commercial and industrial)	17	21	26	29	32	36	34	47	55	41
Commercial and industrial institutes	—	2	2	4	4	4	4	4	4	4
Agricultural schools	—	2	1	2	1	1	2	4	4	5
Elementary schools for arts and crafts	—	5	5	7	7	8	10	10	10	20
Ecclesiastical schools (secondary and high)	8	8	8	8	8	8	8	9	9	9
University	—	—	—	1	1	1	1	1	1	1
Teacher training (university level)	—	—	—	—	—	—	—	—	—	1
Teacher training	2	2	4	9	9	10	10	12	12	15
Schools of qualification for station school teachers	2	2	3	6	6	7	7	8	8	11
Primary teachers' schools	—	—	1	3	3	3	3	3	4	4
Art academy	1	1	1	1	1	1	1	1	1	1
Other[2]	—	7	4	4	7	13	12	8	56	40
TOTAL	2,087	2,131	2,437	2,486	2,704	2,819	3,395	3,675	4,140	4,551

1. Including functional.
2. Others are: social service (secondary, intermediate, high), courses for monitors, courses for nurses, training of teachers for the preparatory course to secondary education, religion, training of civil servants, training outside the official programme.

Source: *Anuário Estatística, Angola,* 1970; Direcçao Provincial dos Serviços de Estatística, Angola.

TABLE 9. Guinea: state of education (1962/63 to 1972/73)

Year	Primary		Secondary	
	Students	Teachers	Students	Teachers
1962/63	11,827	162	987	46
1963/64	11,877	164	874	44
1964/65	12,210	163	1,095	45
1965/66	22,489	192	1,293	42
1966/67	24,099	204	1,039	43
1967/68	24,603	244	1,152	40
1968/69	25,213	315	1,773	111
1969/70	25,854	363	1,919	147
1970/71	32,051	601	2,765	110
1971/72	40,843	803	3,188	158
1972/73[1]	47,626	974	4,033	171

1. In 1973: schools, 108; school posts, 261; schools, 5.
Source: Information dated 12 February 1973 supplied by Repartição Provincial dos Serviços de Educação, Província da Guiné.

sense. It cannot have as its objective the mere spreading of knowledge, but rather the formation of citizens capable of feeling to the full the imperatives of Portuguese life, knowing how to interpret them and making them a constant reality, in order to secure the continuation of the Nation.

The Portuguese language was compulsory and the only one to be used in education. . . .[1]

We must be obstinate, intransigent, and insatiable in the intensification of the use of the Portuguese language.

Indoctrination and acculturation were intensive even in primary education, and continued at all levels. Textbooks throw an interesting light on the new educational policy. Unlike those used before the reform, textbooks were considerably Africanized.[2] They showed African life in rural areas and in the towns. Frequently pictures showed Africans in harmonious relations with whites. This depiction of an African culture and environment is, however, completely swamped by pictures of whites or of Portugal, while moral, religious and historical

1. *Diário de Notícias*, 3 September 1967.
2. For the primary-school textbooks in Angola, see: M. A. Samuels, *Portugal's Africanization of Primary School Textbooks in Angola*, 11th Annual Meeting of African Studies Association, Los Angeles, 1968 (Mimeo.).

issues are dealt with—in Portuguese only—from an exclusively Portuguese point of view.

The covers of the schoolbooks for the third and fourth primary grades showed Portuguese caravelles. The first are entitled *Sails of Christ*; the second have a quotation from Camões, the poet of the Portuguese epic: '. . . and if there were more worlds, they would reach them'. History in the fourth grade covered Portuguese history only. History was the only subject other than Portuguese language and arithmetic upon which the student was questioned in the final examination, a certificate of which was necessary for any Angolan seeking employment other than physical labour. The history of the colonies was mentioned a few times, but only in relation to Portuguese history, e.g. the 'discoveries' of Henry the Navigator, and the 'liberation' of Angola from the Dutch occupation. The geography textbooks of the fourth grade had a picture of the Salazar Bridge in Lisbon on the cover and contained detailed information about Portugal, including its ports, rivers and mountains.

Under a decree of February 1973, only textbooks approved of by the Overseas Minister could be used in primary and secondary teaching. It rejected books which

> . . . show themselves to be in disharmony with the moral tradition of the Country, or with the superior interests and values of the Nation.[1]

> The extent of Africanization of primary school textbooks accurately reflects the current position of Angola in Portuguese official thought. The way in which Africanization has been incorporated reflects an acceptance of Angola as an African entity different in population and geography from what obtains in Portugal. The differences which have been accepted, however, are basically superficial ones. They can be allowed in no way to interfere with the view of a unitary, multicontinental Portugal.[2]

In view of its avowed aims and methods at all levels, it cannot be claimed that Portuguese educational policy was serving to advance the African condition, regardless of whether it resulted in a broadening of education or not—unless the attempted destruction of a people's

1. *Notícias* (Lourenço Marques), 25 February 1973.
2. Samuels, op. cit., p. 12–13.

culture and identity can be counted as an advance. This question will be discussed further in the chapter on culture.

Primary education

It would be outside the scope of this study to attempt a full quantitative and qualitative evaluation of the progress of education since 1961, but it will be useful to examine certain more immediately relevant aspects, using Angola as an example. There are two reasons for selecting Angola. First and mainly, Angola has made the most comprehensive progress of all the colonies and so represents the maximum achievement. Secondly, more up-to-date and detailed data are available on education for Angola than for the other colonies.

Tables 6, 7 and 8 showed a remarkable increase in primary school attendance (from 105,781 in 1960/61 to 392,809 in 1969/70). The rapidity of the increase is explained, however, by the extremely low starting level in 1960/61. In 1970/71 children of school age going to school still represented only little more than half (53.43 per cent).[1] As regards Mozambique, the newspaper *Notícias* of Lourenço Marques (of 29 March 1972) gave the corresponding figure as 30 per cent.

Schools are mainly in cities or in white settlements. For Africans living elsewhere access to education is difficult. An official inquiry was made in all rural zones in Angola in 1971, except for areas to which access was denied by the liberation movements. Its 2,643 inquiries showed that 48.5 per cent of the children of shepherds and 20 per cent of farm children did not go to school in 1969/70 because no facilities were available.

To extend schooling to the rural areas where most Africans live, the 1964 decree established schools which provided a pre-primary class and the first three years of primary education. In general, only full primary schools provide the fourth year. Nevertheless all of the schools are counted in the statistics as primary schools. Teachers for the full primary schools (almost exclusively Europeans or mulattos) attended a two-year teacher training course after completing five years of secondary education; teachers in the others needed only

1. Main source for data quoted: *Trabalhos Preparatórios do IV Plano de Fomento (1974–1979) —Promoçao Social—Educaçao.* Luanda, Serviços de Planeamento e Integraçao Económica, 1972 (Mimeo.). Data from other sources are individually acknowledged.

four years of primary school, and four years of teacher training. During the rapid expansion in Angola in 1962, the lower grades in the latter schools were entrusted to monitors, whose only qualifications were four years of primary school and a two-and-a-half month vocation training class. How low this level of training was can be judged from the fact that only after ten years of teaching ('always with good reports at the annual inspections') could monitors apply to take the examination for teacher posts (though there too, the standard was not high). In 1969/70, most the teachers in the three-year schools, and all the monitors, were African.

It will be seen from Table 10 that, in 1969/70, the average proportion of monitors in all of Angola was 44.6 per cent. The percentages were highest in the rural districts of Lunda and Uíge (70.71 per cent and 71.69 per cent, respectively); in the district of Luanda (including the capital and the main area of white settlement), the proportion was only 6.37 per cent while 74.85 per cent of the teachers were at full primary level, as against 28.75 per cent. Moreover, the better-trained teachers tend to remain in the areas of white settlement. In other words, only 28.85 per cent had the stipulated training. This explains the rapid increase in the number of teachers. Even so, the number remained inadequate, amounting to an average of only 2.1 teachers for schools (1.7 in Mozambique). As many city schools had more teachers than the average, probably not all rural schools had even one trained teacher, e.g. Huambo (see Table 10), over 120 pupils were being taught by monitors only in 1969.[1]

The poor quality of education even at the lowest (i.e. primary) level (the only level that affects most Africans) is reflected in the high rate of examination failures—highest in districts with higher student/teacher ratios and a higher proportion of teachers with a low level of training. Failure rates in 1969/70: Angola 50.3 per cent. Failure rates below average: Luanda 42.7 per cent, Cuanza-Norte 44.45 per cent, Moçâmedes 46.95 per cent, Benguela 47.36 per cent. Failure rates above average: Lunda 56.66 per cent, Uíge 58.5 0per cent, Zaire 58.58 per cent and Cuando-Cubango 60 per cent.

The high ratio of failures is also partly explained by the fact that Portuguese was the only language of instruction allowed. As from pre-primary, African children had first to learn Portuguese, and were

1. *Plano de Desenvolvimento do Distrito do Huambo.* Vol. I: *Caraterizaçao Genérica da Regiao.* Luis Alexandre, Teles Grilo et Alia, 1971.

TABLE 10. Angola: teaching agents on the level of primary education (1969/70)

Districts	Total number of teaching agents	Primary school teachers (%)	Teachers for school posts (%)	Monitors (%)
Benguela	744	30.78	34.54	34.68
Bié	507	14.00	35.50	50.49
Cabinda	441	14.74	28.85	59.41
Cuando-Cubango	112	17.85	23.21	58.93
Cuanza-Norte	426	23.71	28.64	47.65
Cuanza-Sul	474	21.31	40.51	46.62
Huambo	—	—	—	—
Huíla	760	25.00	33.55	41.45
Luanda	911	74.85	18.77	6.37
Lunda	198	15.66	13.64	70.71
Malange	616	16.88	35.39	47.73
Moçâmedes	175	35.43	37.71	26.86
Moxico	270	18.52	28.52	52.16
Uíge	544	12.68	15.63	71.69
Zaire	180	16.67	22.22	61.11
TOTAL	6,283	28.75	26.65	44.60

Source: Serviços de Planeamento e Integração Económica, *Trabalhos Preparatórios de IV Plano de Fomento (1974–1979)*, *Educação*, Luanda, 1972 (mimeo.).

thus at a great disadvantage as compared with Portuguese children. The higher rates of failure occurred in the initial grades. Statistics for Angola are not available but those for Mozambique show a pre-primary failure rate of 67.1 per cent as against an average failure rate of 57.8 per cent.[1] However, transfer from pre-primary to first grade did not depend exclusively on proficiency in Portuguese. As a United Nations document points out:[2]

> Recent events suggest however that an African child who is already 7 years old, who speaks Portuguese fluently and can count in Portuguese, may not be able to enter first grade as a Portuguese child would but may have to go through the pre-primary class, where he will be 'made to acquire the social habits necessary for attending common schools with

1. *Anuário Estatístico de Moçambique 1969*, Instituto Nacional de Estatística, *Delegação de Moçambique*, Lourenço Marques.
2. United Nations document A/6700/Ref. 1 of 1967.

89

the same successes as children from a European type of environment'.

Of all students enrolled in Angola in 1967–70, 4.4 per cent completed primary education, i.e. passed the final examination of the fourth grade. The highest percentage (9.58 per cent) was in Luanda, the lowest in Cuando-Cubango (1.96 per cent). The planners themselves comment:[1]

> The conclusion does not vindicate the system. Most of the population (and nearly all the rural population) attend only the first two, or at most three, grades, leaving school with only the sketchiest of knowledge, rudimentary to such a degree that within a short while they fall back into illiteracy; and the consequences for the economy are those that result from the almost total unproductivity of the investment involved.

We feel that the evidence set out above justifies saying that Portugal's alleged educational achievement in the colonies during the sixties did not reach a reasonable standard, quantitatively or qualitatively, even at the lowest level of education. The examples quoted almost all refer to Angola, where the achievement was greatest. Moreover, despite the continued assertions of racial equality in the colonies, Africans continued to be subject to discrimination in education.

Education at higher levels

The extremely modest expansion at levels above primary during the sixties matched the modesty of their starting point. The planners stated that:[2]

> . . . beyond this limit of primary education, the discouraging break which appears in the rate of schooling can only reflect the failure to provide more general access to secondary or technical education.

Most Africans were debarred by selective processes from access to any education beyond primary level.

1. *Trabalhos Preparatórios do IV Plano de Fomento (1974-1979). Educaçao. Serviços de Planeamento e Integraçao Económica*, p. 20, Luanda, 1972.
2. ibid., p. 71.

Post-primary education was mainly technical and occupational, its object being to produce more skilled Africans. Figures for Mozambique are given in Table 11. At secondary level in 1966/67, 70.2 per cent of the Africans were attending technical or occupational schools and only 29.8 per cent academic schools, whereas most Europeans attended academic schools. Of 444,983 Africans being educated in Mozambique 439,974 were at primary level.

Figures for Africans receiving post-primary education in Angola are not available, since the Angolan statistics no longer distinguish between races. From the totals given in Tables 6, 7 and 8, however, it is easy to deduce that the numbers were insignificant.

The position is prejudiced still further by two factors: facilities were available in only a very few places, usually not very accessible to most Africans; secondly, the small proportion of those who successfully completed post-primary courses made such education appear uneconomic from the official point of view.

There is a strong concentration of schools and pupils in a few districts and particularly in the district of Luanda: in 1970/71, 87.46 per cent of all secondary first-grade students lived in eight of Angola's fifteen districts, with 38.79 per cent of them in the district of Luanda. In the secondary second cycle 77.18 per cent of the students were concentrated in four districts, the district of Luanda alone accounting for 45.65 per cent. The corresponding percentages in secondary complementary courses were 89.6 per cent and 57.95 per cent respectively.

The rate of failure in first-cycle secondary was 40 per cent.

University education in Angola and Mozambique was notional (see Tables 6, 7 and 8, 1,402 students in 1969/70, in Angola. Mozambique (1968/69) had 1,145 students of whom 33 completed their studies. Courses most attended were engineering and medicine (75.94 per cent of students in Angola in 1968/69). Courses providing agronomist, veterinarian and social-service training (which would be very important for rural people and rural development) were less well attended mainly because of the poor propects open to those who qualify.[1]

Separate figures are not given in Angola for Africans studying at universities. According to relatively favourable estimates, the proportion in 1970 was at most 15 per cent.[2] In Mozambique, in 1966/67,

1. *Trabalhos Preparatórios.* . , op. cit.
2. Joachim F. Kahl, *Pro und kontra Portugal*, p. 71, Stuttgart, 1972.

TABLE 11. Mozambique: students enrolled, by type of school and race (1966/67)

Race	Total	Primary (children of school age)	School[1]	Secondary					Higher			Teacher training
				Technical and occupational			Art academy	Seminaries	Universities	Seminaries	Other	
				Commercial, industrial	Agricultural	Other						
Whites	29,200	13,838	7,238	7,037	57	100	315	22	485	2	27	79
Negroes	444,983	439,974	1,076	2,360	64	104	9	544	9	48	2	793
Others	20,811	15,171	1,605	3,797	2	28	39	14	120	—	4	31
TOTAL	494,994	468,983	10,176	13,194	123	232	363	580	614	50	33	903

1. No differentiation by race is made in statistics for students attending secondary school; hence the discrepancy between the total and the sum of the entries in this column.

Source: Província de Moçambique, Estatísticas de Educação 1966/67; Instituto Nacional de Estatística, Direcção Provincial dos Serviços de Estatística. Calculations made by the author.

of 614 students 9 were Africans (cf. Table 11). In 1967/68, of a total of 748, 8 Africans (5 studying medicine and 3 engineering), corresponding to 1.1 per cent of the total; 83.5 per cent were whites.[1] In view of these figures, the figure of 15 per cent given alone for Angola looks like an overestimate.

Among other obstacles, few Africans could afford the basic annual university fee of 1,000 escudos, plus a further 400-650 escudos (depending on the course taken).

Enrolment at the different levels

The extent of school enrolment provides one index to a country's capacity to absorb modern science and technology, with all the implications which that has for socio-economic development. The validity of the index was of course reduced if a high percentage did not complete their studies. A developing country first has to import its scientific knowledge. Education helps to form the skill necessary to adapt that knowledge to the country's needs and, later, to developing its own methods and techniques, as its own economic development proceeds.

> Development must lead, at least in the long run, to the establishment of scientific societies. Indeed, the economic structure and, indirectly, the social structure proper of a developed country tend to become a scientific structure, executing the tasks of production by using, in an increasingly rationalized manner, industrial techniques and processes which need highly qualified manpower and personnel and, at the same time, resources and means which can only be provided by permanent scientific research.[2]

A comparison of Tables 12 and 13 immediately reveals that, in primary education, Angola falls far behind the advanced countries, but also behind some of the developing countries. In view of the high percentage in Angola who do not complete their studies, the gap is probably still greater. At levels other than primary, the comparison shows Angola in a catastrophic situation.

The higher the level of education, the fewer enrolled. This trend

---

1. Eugénio Lisboa, op. cit., p. 296 and 321.
2. *Trabalhos Preparatórios* . . . , op. cit., p. 51.

TABLE 12. Enrolment by district at the different levels of education, 1970/71 (in percentages of the total population)

Districts	Population 1970	Primary	Preparatory Course A	Secondary education B General	Secondary education B Complementary	Total A + B	Middle level[1] 1968/69	Higher level 1968/69
Benguela	474,897	8.52	0.70	0.52	0.10	1.32	—	—
Bié	650,337	7.82	0.15	0.09	0.01	0.25	—	—
Cabinda	80,337	16.72	0.95	0.30	0.04	1.29	—	—
Cuando-Cubango	112,073	6.89	0.12	0.05	—	0.17	—	—
Cuanza-Norte	298,062	6.60	0.39	0.15	—	0.54	—	—
Cuanza-Sul	458,592	5.31	0.27	0.17	0.007	0.447	—	—
Huambo	837,627	8.25	0.40	0.25	0.05	0.70	—	—
Huíla	644,864	5.50	0.29	0.23	0.03	0.55	—	—
Luanda	560,589	10.28	1.95	1.58	0.39	3.92	—	—
Lunda	502,538	3.38	0.04	0.02	—	0.06	—	—
Malange	558,630	7.09	0.28	0.13	0.01	0.42	—	—
Moçâmedes	53,058	10.03	1.52	1.37	0.13	3.02	—	—
Moxico	213,119	7.55	0.19	0.13	0.015	0.33	—	—
Uíge	386,037	9.49	0.25	0.10	—	0.35	—	—
Zaire	41,766	13.36	0.60	—	—	—	—	—
TOTAL	5,673,046	7.74	0.5	0.34	0.06	0.86	0.2	0.2

1. Comprising *institutos comerciais, institutos industriais* and *regentes agrícolas.*
Source: Trabalhos Preparatórios . . ., op. cit.

TABLE 13. School enrolment in various countries (percentage of the total population)

Countries	Population (in thousands)	Primary	Secondary	Higher
Federal Republic of Germany (1959–60)	52,785	9.5	6.9	0.30
Austria (1960–61)	7,049	10.2	4.3	0.55
Czechoslovakia (1960–61)	13,599	15.7	11.4	0.42
Spain (1959–60)	29,662	13.2	2.2	0.25
U.S.S.R. (1960–61)	210,500	14.2	2.5	0.80
United States (1960–61)	164,300	18.4	6.3	1.96
Italy (1958–59)	49,052	9.5	3.6	0.35
Greece (1959–60)	8,173	11.3	3.2	0.29
Netherlands (1960–61)	11,186	13.0	6.5	0.36
Portugal (1959–60)	8,851	9.8	2.2	0.24

Source: Trabalhos Preparatórios . . ., op. cit.

accentuates if we consider the African population alone. Only a few got beyond primary level, and practically none got to university.

Education and science

The implications for science training are obvious. If so few Africans could complete secondary school or attend a university, fewer still could qualify in science or the professions.

It is, therefore, not surprising to find that research scarcely exists in the colonies. Although the Development Plan of the former government recognized that 'a static and passive university limited to teaching belatedly what others have discovered seems inconceivable'[1] nothing was done to create the necessary preconditions to enable the universities to undertake research:[2]

It was considered better to try to secure minimum working conditions and progressively implement projects which turn out to be practicable with the means that the university has at its disposal and the resources of other research agencies. Installations and equipment provided for teaching purposes can also be used for research, without excluding the possi-

1. *III Plano de Fomento para 1968–1973, Presidência do Conselho*, Vol. III, p. 480, Lisbon, 1968.
2. ibid.

bility that, in some cases, it may be necessary to have recourse to independent research facilities.

Consequently, little funds were available for such research: only 5,000 contos out of the 25.3 million contos allocated for Angola under the Third Development Plan.[1]

Research not connected with education was somewhat more favourably treated: an allocation of 652,900 contos under the plan.[2] This, however, was much too little and, with the shortage of scientists and technicians, explained why there was so seldom any scientific performance worth mentioning.

Research in theory was devoted mainly to land surveying (i.e. cartography, hydrology, hydrography) and agriculture (including vetinerary medicine) but in fact was practically confined to agriculture. The Instituto de Investigação Agronómica (founded in 1962) works on specialized crops, forestry, agriculture and cattle-raising.[3]

Starting from the task assigned to them under an FAO programme for establishing comprehensive agricultural statistics, the Missão de Inquéritos Agrícolas de Angola (MIAA) has done excellent work.[4]

> The MIAA is probably at present the only official institution in the Portuguese Overseas Provinces which has a truly detailed knowledge of the economic, social and technical conditions of agriculture in these countries. . . . On the basis of the research done by the MIAA, the widespread view of traditional cattle-raising, as practised by the shepherds in the south of Angola and Mozambique who are blamed for the low yields from their herds, their lack of economic thinking and adherence to a mere subsistence economy, should drastically be revised.

Although only a very small proportion of its research results reached the public, it is already being considered as a model for other agencies, and will certainly play a decisive role in the preparation of the Fourth Development Plan.

A Lisbon Commission covering all the colonies (Comissão Técnica de Planeamento e Integração Económica) called for better basic

1. ibid., p. 496.
2. ibid.
3. ibid., p. 482; and Manfred Kuder, *Angola*, p. 92–3, Darmstadt, 1971.
4. Hermann Pössinger, *Landwirtschaftliche Entwicklung in Angola und Moçambique*, p. 213, München, 1968.

information, and research in economics and sociology. For Mozambique alone it believed an additional fifty graduate agronomists and veterinarians to be necessary. It is difficult to see how they could be provided, since Portugal plus the colonies produce only twenty to twenty-five graduate agronomists a year. The full plan for Mozambique would require an additional 300 graduates in various professions.[1]

In the conditions described above, it could hardly be expected that science would be able to contribute to any notable degree to the development of the colonies. Even if the funds had been available, the educational system was too defective to give any hope of solving the problem of the decisive shortage of skilled people. A Luanda newspaper made the following comments:[2]

> A research institute without research workers. The annual report of the Angola Institute of Medical Research would merit a lament—were not the entire report itself a lament. . . . In the study groups and committees that constitute the machinery of the institution, the work of the past year was practically nil. . . . As far as we know this is not the fault of the Institute and its staff. The Director, in addition to being responsible for the general management, has also to fulfil the duties of several posts; he, an assistant and a single medical doctor form the entire technical personnel! 'Grave problem of senior technical personnel' the report remarks, adding that, from the current year onwards, the situation will become still more critical. . . .

The authorities themselves admitted that research in the colonies was ineffective. Compare the 1970 decree on the reform of research institutes:

> Despite their services to science and culture, their notable contribution to the knowledge of the territories and population, and to the preservation and spread of historical and cultural values, the activities of the Institutes have, in the past few years, suffered from the ineffectiveness of their administration and the lack of incentives for training permanent and devoted research staff who could impart to scientific research, quantitatively and qualitatively, the

1. Pössinger, op. cit., p. 218; and Eugénio Lisboa, op. cit., p. 306–7.
2. *Diário de Lunda*, 9 May 1970.

vigour and dynamism proper to future pathfinders in the constant extension of scientific frontiers.

It is believed that the Institutes have accumulated enough in almost fifteen years of existence to go beyond the stage of the partial measures or the simple experiments used as time went on to remedy the most evident shortcomings of the initial organizational structure. . . .

The aims of the reform were:

To create and maintain the basis for research and the services necessary for them to operate properly; to promote training and refresher courses, and provide opportunities for obtaining degrees through scholarships and grants to persons of proven character and intellectual ability who would later cooperate usefully with the Institutes, or with other official overseas bodies; to help their staffs to improve their qualifications through travel grants, study missions, attendance at scientific meetings, and scholarships; to grant scholarships to graduates, research technicians and assistants; to help the universities as far as possible to participate in research or other appropriate operations in cooperation with the scientific and technical staffs of the Institutes, or by allowing the Institutes to use their laboratories and services; to cooperate with foreign or international organizations in the exchange of information and in making studies which have been authorized by the higher authorities.

Government expenditure on education

The claims made by Portugal (and by some authors) regarding the extent and significance of the educational effort in the colonies during the sixties can be examined in the light of the State expenditure involved. Tables 14-16 show the amounts committed or spent under development plans on education in relation to other items and to total expenditure. Table 17 shows comparitive figures for ordinary and extraordinary expenditure 1960–71.

As can be seen, expenditure on education was a very small portion of government expenditure. This may also be true of most countries; but in a country with such an alarmingly low level of general education, education might be expected to receive a greater preference and

TABLE 14. Angola: Second Development Plan 1959–64. Expenditure on education compared with total expenditure and expenditure on selected items (in thousands contos)

Items	Initial estimate 1959–64	1959–62		1963		1964	
		Planned	Actual	Planned	Actual	Planned	Actual
Education	150.0[1]	110.0[1]	105.5[1]	27.0	...	30.0	...
Industry	60.0	38.0	34.7	13.5	...	21.0	...
Transport and communications	2,238.6	1,725.1	1,390.2	160.0	...	175.0	...
TOTAL	4,713.9	3,406.4	2,655.7	739.5	...	698.0	...

1. Combined data for education and health.   ... = Data not available.
Sources: Plano Intercalar de Fomento 1965–67, Presidência do Conselho, Lisbon, Vol. III; *Banco de Angola, Boletim Trimestral*, No. 24, Outubro-Dezembro 1963; *Banco de Angola, Relatório e Contas, Exercício de 1962.*

TABLE 15. Angola: Transitional Development Plan 1965–67. Expenditure on education, compared with total expenditure and expenditure on selected items (in thousand contos)[1]

Item	Initial estimate 1965–67	1965		1966		1967	
		Planned	Actual	Planned	Actual	Planned	Actual
Education	540.0	40.0	39.4	40.0	38.3	35.0	30.1
Industry	2,068.0	137.0	31.1	98.6	37.2	270.2	35.6
Transport and communications	1,930.0	349.3	325.3	384.6	376.3	431.1	354.7
TOTAL	7,210.0	1,000.1	752.4	947.0	844.0	1,191.0	775.7

1. Planned figures are adjusted figures.
Sources: Plano Intercalar de Fomento 1965–67, Presidência do Conselho, Vol. II; *Banco de Angola, Relatório e Contas, Exercício de 1967; Relatório da Execuçao do Plano Intercalar de Fomento, Ultramar; Presidência do Conselho, 1965, 1966, 1967;* Serviços de Planeamento e Integraçao Económica, *Trabalhos Preparatórios do IV Plano de Fomento (1974–1979); Educaçao*, Luanda, 1972 (mimeo.).

be the subject of a greater financial effort. This is not the case in the Portuguese colonies.

Total government expenditure increased rapidly during the sixties and especially after 1967. Expenditure on education shows nothing like a corresponding increase (see Fig. 1). This failure was particularly serious so far as the development plans were concerned. These would normally be expected to give first preference to

Continued page 104

99

TABLE 16. Angola: Third Development Plan 1968–73. Expenditure on education compared with total expenditure and expenditure on selected items (in thousand contos)

Items	Initial estimate 1968–73	1968		1969		1970		1971	
		Planned	Actual	Planned	Actual	Planned	Actual	Planned	Actual
Education	700.0	67.0	66.2	117.9	110.8	94.4	89.5	133.0	n
Industry	14,960.1	141.0	139.9	47.8	44.0	106.3	104.4	44.0	n
Transport and communications	3,778.8	751.8	737.1	622.9	593.7	675.8	615.1	450.7	n
TOTAL	25,383.5	1,450.7	1,351.5	1,439.2	1,201.9	1,532.4	1,346.3	1,174.0	n

n = data not yet published.

Sources: *Terceiro Plano do Fomento 1968–1973*, Presidencia do Conselho, Vol. III; *Síntese das Actividades dos Serviços 1967–68*: Secretaria Provincial de Educaçao, Angola; *Terceiro Plano de Fomento, Relatório da Execuçao em 1969*, Ultramar, Presidencia do Conselho; *Terceiro Plano de Fomento, Programas de Execuçao 1968–1971*, Ultramar, Presidencia do Conselho; Provincia de Angola, Contas de Gerencia e do Exercicio de 1970, Direcçao dos Serviços de Fazenda e Contabilidade; Serviços de Planeamento e Integraçao Económica, *Trabalhos Preparatórios do IV Plano de Fomento (1974–1979), Educaçao*, Luanda, 1972 (mimeo.).

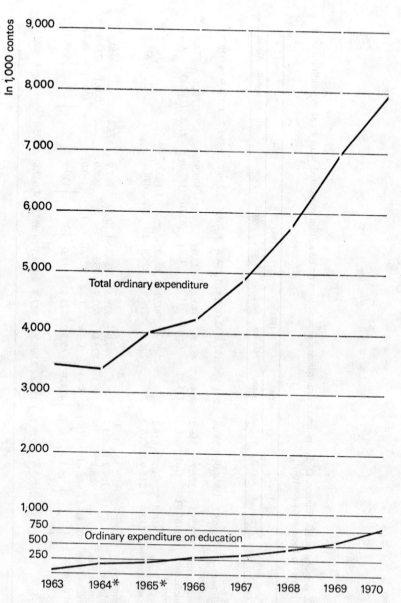

Fig. 1. Angola: public finances (1963–70). Ordinary expenditure on education compared with total ordinary expenditure. The asterisk (*) denotes budget figures for education expenditure.

TABLE 17. Angola: public finance. Ordinary and extraordinary expenditure on education compared with total expenditure and selected items (in thousands contos)[1]

Items	1960 Planned	1960 Actual	1961 Planned	1961 Actual	1962 Planned	1962 Actual	1963 Planned	1963 Actual	1964 Planned	1964 Actual	1965 Planned	1965 Actual
Ordinary expenditure	1,868.7	1,868.0	1,885.8	1,891.1	2,197.8	2,099.4	3,286.6	3,465.4	3,229.7	3,399.7	4,371.9	4,028.3
General administration and control	322.3	272.7	356.2	304.3	482.8	440.3	543.0	...	595.9	...	711.6	711.5
(Of which education)	(...)	(84.0)	(...)	(35.5)	(...)	(...)	(...)	(62.0)	(175.0)	(...)	(192.1)	(...)
Development services	648.8	...	616.2	...	748.9	702.7	1,308.3	...	1,163.6	...	...	1,607.5
Military services	212.6	215.9	208.2	...	206.0	219.9	356.9	...	474.4	...	...	615.8
Extraordinary expenditure	...	764.2	873.1	1,226.5	794.9	928.3	854.5	1,206.9	817.9	875.4	...	940.8
Development plan	...	688.1	...	748.1	725.0	602.7	739.5	...	698.0	...	1,000.1	752.4
(Of which education)	(...)	(...)	(...)	(...)	(...)	(...)	(27.0)	(...)	(30.0)	(...)	(40.0)	(39.4)
National defence	{ ...	{ 76.1	{ ...	{ 478.3[2]	{ 69.9	{ 325.5	{ 115.0	{ ...	{ 119.9	{ ...	{ ...	{ 188.4
Other												
TOTAL	2,633.0	2,632.9	2,758.9	3,117.6	2,992.8	3,027.7	4,141.1	4,672.0	4,047.6	4,275.1	...	4,969.1

Items	1966 Planned	1966 Actual	1967 Planned	1967 Actual	1968 Planned	1968 Actual	1969 Planned	1969 Actual	1970 Planned	1970 Actual	1971 Planned	1971 Actual
Ordinary expenditure	4,430.5[3]	4,187.3	4,247.4	4,839.1	5,164.8	5,755.9	...	6,941.2	6,836.0	7,930.0	8,690.0	...
General administration and control	896.9	806.8	945.7	944.6	1,193.9	1,146.3	...	1,596.8	1,847.0	2,036.0	2,363.2	...
(Of which education)	(242.0)	(261.6)	(263.6)	(305.9)	(384.4)	(393.4)	(498.9)	(574.3)	(602.8)	(780.7)	(847.2)	(...)
Development services	1,553.2	1,503.4	1,203.6	1,628.0	1,593.8	2,141.6	...	2,580.2	2,423.0	2,952.0	3,097.6	...
Military services	662.6		782.0	862.4	800.9	809.9	...	846.6	686.0	862.0	796.1	...
Extraordinary expenditure	1,273.7	1,163.7	1,274.8	1,059.4	1,461.0	1,892.9	...	2,025.9	...	2,360.0	1,907.4	...
Development plan	947.0	844.0	1,191.0	775.7	1,450.7	1,351.5	1,439.2	1,201.8	1,532.4	1,344.3	1,174.0	...
(Of which education)	(40.0)	(38.3)	(35.0)	(30.1)	(67.0)	(66.2)	(117.9)	(110.8)	(94.4)	(89.5)	(133.0)	...
National defence	} 128.9	} 319.7	} 137.3	} 283.7	} 115.0	} 541.3	...	450.0	425.0	545.0	450.0	...
Other							...	374.0	534.0	468.0	283.4	...
TOTAL	5,704.2	5,351.1	5,552.3	5,898.6	6,625.8	7,648.8	...	8,967.1	8,690.0	10,290.0	10,598.3	...

1. Because of the difficulty of access to uniform sources, the global figures are not in all cases identical with the sum of the single items as given in the columns, e.g. even if no special note is added, the single items may include additional credits that were taken up during the course of the year; thus the sum of the individual items may be higher than the global sum as given is the table.

2. Mainly military expenses 'because of action in the north of the province' (see: *Banco de Angola, Relatório, Relatório e Contas, 1967*).

3. Includes credits opened in the course of the year.

... = Data not available.

Sources: Relatório e Contas do Banco de Angola, 1962, 1963, 1966–68, Banco de Angola, *Economic and Financial Survey*, Luanda, 1970, *Relatório da Execução do Plano Intercalar de Fomento*, Ultramar, Presidência do Conselho, 1967. *Anuário Estatístico, Vol. II*, 1968–1970, Lisbon, I.N.E. *Boletim Oficial de Angola, F Série, Budget da Província*, 1971. *Província de Angola, Contas da Gerência e do Exercício de 1970, Direcção dos Serviços de Fazenda e Contabilidade*, Luanda, 1971. Serviços de Planeamento e Integração Económica, *Trabalhos Preparatórios do IV Plano de Fomento (1974–1979), Educação*, Luanda, 1972. United Nations General Assembly, Documents A/6300/Add.3 (part I) of November 1966, A/6700/Rev.1 1967, A/7623/Add.3 September 1969, A/8023/Add.3 October 1970.

education, universally accepted as one of the basic prerequisites for development. Ordinary and extraordinary government expenditure, on the contrary, were used mainly to further military aims, and infrastructure and industrial projects served the export-oriented economy of the colonies. The advantages went to the Portuguese economy, and certainly not to the African populations of the colonies.

In considering public expenditure on education, an essential point is the *per capita* expenditure on the education of each student.

From Table 18 we discover that, as in all countries, government investment per student is enormously higher at university level than at all the others; and this is mainly responsible for the *per capita*

TABLE 18. Angola: increase of government expenditure per student (in escudos)

	1966/67	1967/68	1968/69	1969/70
General	1,069	1,235	1,594	1,848
General (non-university)	952	1,002	1,002	1,002
University	60,000	93,623	95,310	126,218

Source: Trabalhos Preparatórios . . ., op. cit.

increase, the increase at other levels being almost nil. It will be recalled that Africans had practically no access to the university, which was reserved almost exclusively for the Portuguese (cf. the claim that the educational system in the colonies did not discriminate against Africans). Advanced education was élitist, and was given preferential treatment by the State. The ratio of *per capita* expenditure at university to other levels was approximately 1 : 60 in 1966/67, rising to 1.8 : 126 in 1969/70.

4   Conclusions

At the end of this part it seems reasonable to conclude that, prior to 1961, the achievements of Portuguese colonialism in education can scarcely be called either quantitatively or qualitatively impressive. It can also be said that the educational policy in the colonies since the beginning of the sixties did not seek to advance the African population; that the considerable quantitative improvement during the sixties had not been at all levels, but only at the lowest, i.e. in primary education; that the standard reached was still very low; that qualitative progress was small, and particularly so with regard to the education of Africans; that Africans were still discriminated against in education by social and financial barriers, and that access to education was made especially difficult at the secondary and higher levels; that there was practically no African participation in the scientific activities of the colonies; that the State had done practically nothing about research; and that the extent of the State's financial investment in education and science afford little evidence of a concern for education in the colonies and, hence, for the education of the African population.

Such efforts as Portugal made to provide education for Africans were imposed by the development needs of Portuguese colonialism itself, by the international situation, and in particular by the demonstration the liberation movements provided of an alternative to Portuguese domination. Portugal did undoubtedly succeed in forming an African élite which, though few in numbers, provided an African petty *bourgeoisie*, and encouraged African officials and small-scale managers to ally themselves with Portugal. The need for such managers could lead to a neo-colonialist solution which could then be regarded as a 'success' for Portuguese educational policy;

but would certainly do little to improve the status of the African populations.

During the preparatory work for the fourth plan, review was made of educational policy:[1]

> From the analyses of the Development Plans which were valid in the sixties, and from speeches of those responsible at the highest level for education in Angola (the only documents that make any reference to the subject) it becomes very clear that the major aim of educational policy was to make the Portuguese language the universal vehicle of communication. This was to be done by mass schooling, and by giving vast numbers a superficial knowledge of reading and writing. This acculturation was meant to show the world a multiracial society, enjoying the unity of teaching and education which the identity of programmes provides for—in sum, the Portuguezation of the native communities, which the Portuguese Youth Movement encourages by setting up vocational schools, and courses of nationalist education.

The former Provincial Secretary for Education in Angola could accordingly only have been writing with tongue in cheek in his preface to a book on the history of education in Angola, although he is right in saying that it is in the light of the education it provides that the real intentions of a civilizing people can be judged:[2]

> In the matter of relations between Europeans and coloured peoples, it cannot be denied that we are the only ones whose ideas and solutions have remained unaltered overseas since the very beginning. We have a mountain of irrefutable historical documents that prove this. Of this, everything which, despite many blows of fate in changing internal and external conditions, we have done in regard to teaching education, everywhere we have set foot is, strictly speaking, the undeniable proof. Indeed, it is from what a civilizing nation does in regard to teaching and education overseas that the true nature of its intentions can be learnt.

1. *Trabalhos Preparatórios* . . . , op. cit., p. 5.
2. Martins dos Santos, op. cit., p. 7.

Appendix

Basic legislation on the various levels and kinds of education overseas [1]

Primary education—reform of primary education overseas
Decreto-Lei No. 45 908 de 10 Setembro de 1964

Preparatory cycle of secondary education
Installation of the cycle: *Decreto-Lei No. 47 480, de 2/1/67.*
Installation of the cycle overseas: *Portaria No. 22 944, de 4/10/67.*
Alterations: *Decreto-Lei No. 48 541, de 23/8/68.*
Statute: *Decreto No. 48 572, de 9/9/68.*
Programmes: *Portaria No. 23 601, de 9/9/68.*

Secondary schools (lyceums)
Reform: *Decreto-Lei No. 36 507, de 17/9/47.*
Statute: *Decreto No. 36 508, de 17/9/47.*

Technical occupational education
Reform: *Decreto-Lei No. 37 028, de 25/8/48.*
Statute: *Decreto No. 37 029, de 25/8/48.*

Agricultural education
Regulation of agricultural education at intermediate level: *Decreto No. 38 026, de 2/11/50,* applied to Angola by *Portaria No. 20 918, de 17/11/64* (supplementing *Portaria No. 16 003, de 15/10/56).*
Portaria No. 21 411, de 23/7/65 which applies overseas the bases XVII and XXI of the *Lei No. 2 025, de 19/6/47.*
Programmes of the secondary courses in agriculture: *Portaria No. 21 848, de 1/2/66.*
Programmes of elementary courses in agriculture: *Portaria No. 21 782, de 12/1/66.*

---

1. Information contained in a letter dated 24 April 1973 from the Ministario do Ultramar, Direcção-General de Educação. Lisbon.

Reorganization of agricultural education overseas: *Decreto No. 47 198, de 14/9/66.*

Regulation of the practical schools of agriculture: *Decreto No. 41 382,* applied by *Portaria No. 22 577, de 16/3/67.*

Regulation of elementary agricultural schools in Mozambique: *Decreto-Lei No. 3 048, de 24/11/70.*

Education at intermediate level

Primary teacher training schools: *Decreto No. 32 243,* to be applied overseas according to *Portaria No. 19 112* and *Decreto-Leis No. 43 369 e 49 406, de 24/11/69.*

Regulation of industrial and commercial institutes approved by *Decretos Nos. 38 032 e 38 031, de 4/11/50* and *23/4/51;* some articles are altered by *Decreto No. 38 899* applied overseas under *Portaria No. 199/70, de 21/4/70.*

Schools for the training of sports teachers

Decreto-Lei No. 49 238, de 11/9/69, applied by *Portaria No. 600/70, de 23/12/70.*

Portaria No. 60/71, de 6/2/71—approves the regulations of the teacher training courses.

Vocational schools (escolas de artes e ofícios)

Decreto No. 422/71, de 1/10/71.

Schools for the training of teachers for three-year primary schools

Decreto-Lei No. 45 908, de 10/9/64.

Teaching (estágios pedagógicos)

Preparatory cycle, secondary education: *Decreto-Lei No. 49 119, de 14/7/69.*

Lyceum: *Decreto-Lei No. 48 868, de 17/2/69 e 49 204, de 25/8/69,* applied overseas under *Portaria No. 24 380, de 21/10/69.*

Technical-occupational education: *Decreto No. 49 205, de 25/8/69,* applied overseas under *Portaria No. 119/70, de 24/2/70.*

III Culture

1 Culture: a general survey

The effects of Portuguese colonialism on the cultures of all the dominated peoples have one common denominator: they all stem from colonial relationships, i.e. relationships between dominator and dominated, exploiter and exploited. However, there are differences deriving from the different forms which colonialism may take, e.g. whether the main purpose is settlement (Angola, Mozambique) or economic exploitation (Guinea, Cape Verde, São Tomé and Príncipe).[1]

> The colonization by settlement tends to substitute the autochthonous element, its institutions, its economy, its culture by another human element foreign to the country, better equipped than the former, occasionally very numerous, in any case prevalent in the political plane and aimed at prolonging within the colony, for itself exclusively, the social and juridical apparatus of civilization and the modes of life of its metropolis.

The colonized society sees its structures becoming outmoded in the long run and reaches socio-cultural stagnation; its living space is reduced and its accomplishments are systematically denigrated.

Where the colonies are mainly for economic exploitation, the Portuguese presence tends to be limited to colonial officials and a few traders. The local society is left largely undisturbed and there is much less interference with its culture. Traditional cultural values are

---

1. M. Lacheraf, 'Les Diverses Formes de la Domination Coloniale et de son Impact sur le Terrain Socio-culturel des Pays Colonisés ou en Voie de Développement' (contribution to the Unesco Meeting of Experts on the Influence of Colonialism on the Artist, his Milieu, and his Public in Developing Countries, Dar-es-Salaam, 5–10 July 1972).

even encouraged, seemingly out of respect, but also as providing an effective curb on local progress.

Legitimization . . .

Portugal, like all the other colonial powers, tried to legitimize domination of the colonial territories as the fulfilment of a social duty.

Eventualy it was denied that economic advantage was the main motive. The riches of the colonies obviously benefited the metropolis, but this was represented as merely a secondary result. Compare former Prime Minister Marcello Caetano:[1]

> Portuguese concern for the natives was evident from the first centuries in the desire to bring them the message of the Gospel, extricate them from the darkness of paganism, and save their souls.
>
> In doing so, the Portuguese at the same time saw the possibility of taking advantage of the unutilized riches of the new worlds, of enhancing the worth of these countries and of giving Europe a share in the unheard-of opportunities offered by these tropical regions.

Indeed, Portugal has always associated the Catholic Church closely with her 'duty to colonize' and educate the colonial peoples in the particular standards of Portuguese culture. A minimum of Europeanization was necessary in order to impose a social order that facilitated economic exploitation. On the other hand, if Africans assimilated European culture and techniques too successfully, they might pose a threat to colonial domination. The Catholic Church helped to secure the advantages of the former without running the risk of the latter by co-operating in a strictly limited and controlled acculturation; the 'native' received enough of 'white culture' and Christian principles to make him obedient and disciplined, but not enough to enable him to become skilled, independent-minded and active.[2]

1. Marcello Caetano, *Tradiçoes, Princípios e Métodos da Colonizaçao Portuguesa*, Lisbon, 1951.
2. For the role of the Catholic Church, see: Eduardo Mondlane, 'Nationalisme et Développement, Thèse présentée au Projet "Brazil-Portuguese Africa" de l'Université de Califournie, 27–28 février 1968', *Colonies Portugaises: La Victoire ou la Mort, Tricontinental*, p. 80–4, Havanna, 1970; and Perry Anderson, *Portugal e o Fim do Ultracolonialismo*, p. 66–72, Rio de Janeiro, 1966.

In his Christmas Message of 1960, the Patriarch of Lisbon, Cardinal Cerejeira, stated:[1]

> We need schools in Africa, but schools in which we show the native the way to the dignity of man and the glory of the Nation that protects him. . . . We want to teach the natives to write, to read and to count, but not make them doctors.

The general anticolonialist movement throughout the world brought about a change in internationally accepted ethical standards on the subject. Portugal had to alter her case accordingly, supplementing the argument of 'spreading the faith' with new sociological reasons and the necessity of spreading Portugal's advanced culture to the 'primitive peoples' of the colonies. A quotation from a decree of 1940—'The native must gradually be brought from his wild condition to civilized life'[2]—prefigures what Salazar said in 1957:[3]

> We believe that there are decadent or—if you prefer—backward races whom we feel we have a duty to lead to civilization—a task of forming human beings that must be undertaken in a humane manner. That we do feel and act in this way is demonstrated by the fact that there is no network of hatred and subversive organizations wanting to reject Portuguese sovereignty and take it over. This state of affairs, verified and reported by all observers, explained most likely by the profound human contact in the relations between Portuguese and native everywhere, and even with a certain mutual penetration of cultures, in so far as it can be said that local culture existed.

These words were spoken four years before the beginning of the armed revolt in Angola. Portugal then deemed it increasingly necessary to talk about the 'peaceful co-existence of the races', with the emphasis on 'assimilation'.[4]

> Although the Portuguese respect the way of life of the natives, they have always tried to induct them into Portuguese culture

1. Joachim F. Kahl, *Pro und kontra Portugal. Der Konflikt um Angola und Mosambik*, p. 173–4, Stuttgart, 1972.
2. Decree No. 238 of 15 May 1940.
3. Radio address of 1 November 1957.
4. Caetano, *Tradiçoes . . .* , op. cit. (Lusitania = Portugal).

and civilization and thus bring them into the Lusitanian community.

The idea of the Portuguese 'instinctive vocation' for civilizing other peoples in tropical areas was developed by the Brazilian historian Gilberto Freyre into a full-scale theory of 'Luso-Tropicalism'. Though Freyre bases his observations on Brazil, the Portuguese Government found them useful as propaganda for its policy of assimilating Africans.

The assimilation policy

The policy of assimilation was based on Portugal's claim to be non-racist: anyone in the colonies could absorb Portuguese civilization and be regarded as equal to the Portuguese by birth, without distinction of colour or birth, i.e. Africans could become Portuguese through the medium of the Catholic religion, the Portuguese language and technology. From 1961, the former government also tried to achieve assimilation in Angola and Mozambique by means of European colonization. Compare the Preamble to the Second Plan (1959–64):[1]

The Portuguese colonist deems himself to be performing a mission of national importance which at this time transcends merely national interests. In present circumstances the conclusion is inescapable that the mission of the centuries should be intensified; our planning must not fail to take into account the necessity of multiplying overseas the agents of this way of life, ensuring the creation of the economic and administrative structures necessary to accelerate the influx of colonists, those to whom the task of assimilation, by word, deed, and example, mainly falls. . . . We must therefore people Africa with Europeans who can assure the stability of our sovereignty and promote the Portuguesation of the native population.

The claim to be non-racist, however, is disproved by the very basis of the assimilation policy. To be 'assimilated' means to be regarded as belonging to the 'civilized' population, this criterion originally being restricted to the whites. Since the distinction between 'civilized' and 'non-civilized' is made along racial lines, it is difficult to consider this a

1. Allison Butler Herrick, *et al.*, *Area Handbook for Mozambique*, p. 189, Washington, 1969.

non-racist attitude. Efforts were made to disguise the racism by assigning a cultural aspect: the African was accepted as civilized, and incorporated into Portuguese society if he reached a certain cultural level which included the ability to read and write Portuguese. In view of the high percentage of illiteracy among the Portuguese settlers in the colonies, it is difficult to see why they also were not counted among the 'non-civilized', unless it is admitted that the distinction was in fact made on grounds of race, and not of culture.

But the 'generosity' of allowing Africans to become 'more civilized' and thus—theoretically at least—to enjoy the same rights as the other Portuguese was of very limited relevance in view of the obstacles that prevented the African from achieving this status. As we have seen, few Africans could obtain or afford the education needed. Compare the 'assimilated' figures: 30,000 out of a population of 4 million Africans in Angola in 1950; 4,300 out 5.6 million in Mozambique; and 1,500 out of 503,000 in Guinea.[1]

The other, non-assimilated Africans, had no civil rights. The formal abolition of the *estutato dos indígenas* in 1961 (i.e. immediately after the beginning of the armed struggle in Angola) in practice changed nothing. All Africans in the colonies were declared to be full Portuguese citizens but were issued with different kinds of identity cards. A United Nations report explains:[2]

> The witness Sharfudine Khan has declared that the Mozambican indigenous are not allowed to move without a *caderneta do indígena* or card of identity, in spite of the abolition of the law called *Estatuto do indígena*. The Africans must obtain an authorization from the Portuguese authorities for moving from one district to another in Mozambique as well as in other territories under Portuguese administration. . . . The Rev. McInnes has quoted a letter which he had received from Angola in 1969, telling him that the restrictions imposed with regard to movement and work were even more severe than two years before. No black Angolan had the right to leave the region without a travel permit (*guia*). Before, those who were in possession of an identity card had not needed one, at least theoretically. At the moment, every indigenous must stay hours and sometimes days waiting in the bureaux of the administration in order to obtain a *guia* for whatever

1. *Anuário Estatístico do Ultramar 1958*, Lisbon, Instituto Nacional de Estatística.
2. United Nations document E/CN.4/1050 of 2 February 1971.

kind of movement. According to the witness, the Africans were forced very frequently to obtain these travel permits for presenting them to the police station of the place where they went and to show them again upon their return to prove that these permits had been presented at their destination. The statements of Rev. McInnes with respect to the travel restrictions and to the system of travel permits established by the Portuguese in Africa seem to have been confirmed by the witness Francisco Alexandre.

Colonialist Portugal thus had everything to gain in proclaiming a policy of assimilation which could not possibly work and thus presented no danger; and had moreover the additional advantage of creating an élite who shared the point of view of the colonizers and were thus prepared to assist them in destroying the culture of their own people.

Cultural resistance

The assimilation policy indicated that Portugal had not succeeded in destroying or even essentially weakening the culture of the African peoples.[1] By orally transmitting their literature and by means of popular songs, the Africans succeeded in defending their own languages and continued to use them. Their culture did not remain completely untouched, but it has undoubtedly survived the impact of Portuguese colonization.

Traditional songs continue to give expression to the bitterness of the defeat. The Cuanhamas of Angola have this song:

> I shall give no water to the whites;
> I shall not offer them my gourd.
> For they have killed our king
> They have mutilated our sovereign—
> The king for whom we lay down animal skins.

And the Chope of Mozambique remember being dispossessed of their lands:[2]

---

1. See Amilcar Cabral, 'The Role of Culture in the Struggle for Independence' (contribution to Unesco Meeting of Experts on the Concept of Race, Identity and Dignity, Paris, 3–7 July 1972).
2. Mondlane, op. cit., p. 203–4.

We are still trembling with anger—
It is always the same story
The elder daughters must carry the burden
Natanele tells the white man: leave me in peace
Natanele tells the white man: leave him in peace
And you old men take on interest in our affairs—
For the man whom the white man have named
Is a son of a bitch
The Chope have lost their right to their ancestral lands
Let me tell you . . . .

In most Bantu tribes, it is the responsibility of the elder to hand down to the younger generation in the form of tales the experiences of their ancestors. As Hampate Ba has said: 'Any old man who dies is a burning library'.[1]

Traditional art, subjected to European pressures and influences, continued to resist.[2]

Even in the arts there is a conscious protest against the Portuguese culture. This can be seen in particular in certain Makonde sculptures. Under the influence of the Catholic missionaries, Christ, the Madonna, and the priests have become frequent subjects of Makonde art. Normally they seem in logic and conviction to be imitations of European models. But, occasionally, one can see the subject dealt with differently: the artist has worked in his own doubts or his hostile reaction to the new religion. At first glance, a Madonna seems entirely conventional but, looking a little closer, it can be seen that she carries a wild animal or a demon in place of the infant Jesus; a priest has a serpend under his surplice; the hands and feet of a religious personality are transformed into the claws of a monster. Sometimes a Madonna or Christ is represented as standing upright, trampling on the people.

The instruments of acculturation

Nevertheless, the culture of the African peoples has been deeply affected by the impact of Portuguese colonialism.[3]

1. Virgilio Lemos, 'Das kulturelle Leben Portugiesisch-Afrikas', *Sonderbeilage zur Zeitschrift Afrika heute*, No. 7, 15 April 1965.
2. Mondlane, op. cit., p. 204–5.
3. Basil Davidson, *Angola in the Eye of the Storm*, p. 149, 1972.

The colonial decades resulted in a profound dismantling of the traditional modes of living and subsisting. We have already mentioned certain reasons for this: the intensive use of African labour outside the rural African economy; the imposition of commercialized cultures on exactly such an economy and its effect on the impoverishment of the Africans; the abolition of any form of indigenous government, modest as it may be; the abusive practices of the poor settlers who themselves lived hardly above the subsistence level; and the still more abusive practices of the rich settlers whose plantations needed forced labour in constantly increasing numbers, because they were increasingly ruinous.

The deepest influences were Christian, because the Catholic missionaries were most active and most closely in contact with the African population. In music, songs and the arts, there is frequently a mixture of Christian and African motifs. A good example is provided by the funerary sculture of the Bakongo area in Angola:[1]

> Sand and plaster tombs constructed for important persons were painted in bright colours. The tombs mixed Christain and African motifs and were constructed in the shape of airplanes and automobiles, with the deceased placed inside.

In Mozambique, Makonde carving is outstanding for its expressiveness and technique, although[2]

> Makonde carvings in black wood and ivory have fallen a victim to the adverse influence of the missionaries in the Mueda area, and partly lost their particular expressiveness.

The Madonnas described above are one example of this. Music, dances, poetry and carvings were more radically modified as expressions of the values and concepts of a particular society in the settlement than in the 'economic exploitation' colonies—increasingly so as the colonial administration gained a footing, a capitalist economy was introduced and the moving of social groups started a process of detribalization. A culture is a complex unity; the destruction of parts

1. Allison Butler Herrick *et al.*, op. cit., p. 174.
2. Lemos, op. cit., p. 8.

of it destroys its equilibrium and this is reflected in modifications of form and content.[1]

African culture was strangled by systematically preventing any kind of cultural meeting among the population. A United Nations report describes how this was done under the former policy:[2]

> In his oral statement which is based upon the letters which had been addressed to him in 1969 by friends working in the region of Vila da Ponte in Angola, the Rev. McInnes indicated that the methods of intimidation and the restrictive measures with respect to the freedom of association and expression in Angola had recently been reinforced. . . . The witness João Baptista Nguvulo declared that freedom of expression did not exist in Angola and that the meetings, even those which had a religious character, were not allowed unless whites were present. Another witness, Sharfudine Khan, declared that the Africans were not allowed to have meetings of any sort which were organized particularly for the autochthons of Mozambique and other territories. . . .

In regard to the individual African, the aim of colonial policy was to make him lose his identity, to 'colonize him mentally'. According to Article 68 of the Missionary Statute, the native must be educated 'nationally' and the curricula embraces his complete 'nationalization' and the whole of his moral education.[3]

> The pupil, the school child, has no point of reference other than Portugal in seeking his intellectual identity. The geography of Portugal situates him in space and Portuguese history situates him in time. Although religion holds an important place in keeping the masses subjugated, science plays a fundamental role in improving the methods used to exploit and alienate the masses, while culture becomes yet another gadget, something to entertain the exploiting strata and to fill their leisure time. It is even an anti-culture, a means for dehumanising man. For example, colonialism, which once brought us missionary puritanism, is now giving

1. See Mário de Andrade, *Colonialisme, Culture et Révolution, Tricontinental*, Vol, 13, July-August 1969.
2. United Nations document E/CN.4/1050, op. cit., p. 219–20.
3. Armando Gueboza and Sérgio Vieira, 'Quelques Observations sur la Transformation Culturelle dans le Cadre de la Révolution Mozambicaine' (contribution to Unesco Meeting of Experts on the Influence of Colonialism on the Artist, his Milieu and his Public in Developing Countries, Dar es Salaam, 5–10 July 1972).

us commercialised sex. This anti-culture is definitely intended to create a subjugated society in which selfishness and corruption take their most extreme forms, the better to maintain capitalist and foreign exploitation.

One of the principal instruments of Portuguese colonialism for impressing its culture was the repression of the African languages simultaneously with the spreading of Portuguese. It is assessed as follows in the book on Guinea by the Institute for Overseas Studies:[1]

When the twelve million Portuguese who live in Africa and the other millions throughout the world speak, write and exchange ideas in Portuguese, think and feel in Portuguese, pray in Portuguese, the community will automatically consolidate itself, and spontaneous solidarity will appear— like the flash-over from a spark.

On the armed resistance of the peoples of the colonies, the book says:[2]

Terrorism by fire and sword must be annihilated by military action. This is indispensable and perhaps crushing. But the final battle, with a hundred per cent yield, is the battle of the Portuguese language. With victory here, the Nation forges its best weapon.

Cultural dualism

The policy of assimilation leads to what Mário de Andrade calls 'cultural dualism'. On one side, the large rural population bears the consequences of a foreign economic system and are forced to place their labour at the disposal of the capitalist economy; but they retain the essential characteristics of their own culture. In the urban areas, on the other hand, the higher social strata tend to integrate with the colonial system and are used by the colonizer to propagate Portuguese culture. These are what Cabral has called the native petty *bourgeoisie*. He describes the dualism as follows:[3]

We find then that the great rural masses and a large fraction

---

1. Instituto Supérior de Ciências Sociais e Política Ultramarina, *Cabo Verde, Guiné, São Tomé e Principe*, Curso de Extensao Universitária Ano Lectivo de 1965-1966, Lisbon, p. 717.
2. Ibid., p. 718.
3. Cabral, op. cit.

of the urban population—making up a total of over 99% of the indigenous population—remain apart, or almost so, from any cultural influence by the colonial power. This situation derives on the one hand from the necessarily obscurantist character of imperialist rule which, while despising and repressing the culture of the dominated people, has no interest in promoting acculturation of the masses —the source of forced labour and the prime object of exploitation. On the other hand it derives from the effective cultural resistance of those masses who, subjected to political rule and economic exploitation, find in their own culture the one bulwark strong enough to preserve their identity. Where the native society has a vertical structure, this defence of the cultural heritage is further reinforced by the colonial power's interest in protecting and strengthening the cultural influence of the dominant classes, its allies.

The fact that the dualism exists shows, however, that colonialism failed in one of its aims—the destruction of the indigenous culture. Mário de Andrade writes of language, for example:[1]

> In the rural centres which are seldom visited by Portuguese, the local languages generally maintained themselves intact. As human contacts between the colonial and the colonized are limited almost entirely to relationships of exploitation, it is scarcely possible for osmosis typical of the towns to develop.

The 'return to the sources'

Thus, the colonized population was not alienated from its culture, but only a small assimilated stratum which was in constant contact with the colonial administrative machinery and held an intermediate position in the rural areas between the foreign rulers and the people. This native petty *bourgeoisie*[2]

> . . . usually aspire to a way of life similar to, if not identical with, that of the foreign minority. They limit their intercourse with the masses and at the same time try to become integrated with that minority, often to the detriment of

1. Andrade, op. cit., p. 86.
2. Cabral, op. cit.

family or ethnic bonds and always at personal cost. But, whatever the seeming exceptions, they do not succeed in crossing the barriers imposed by the system. They are prisoners to the contradictions of the social and cultural reality they live in, for they cannot escape, under 'colonial peace', their condition as a marginal or 'marginalized' class. Both *in loco* and within the diasporas implanted in the colonialist metropolis, this 'marginality' constitutes the socio-cultural drama of the colonial elites or native 'petite bourgeoisie', a drama lived more or less intensely according to material conditions and level of acculturation, but always on the individual, not the community, level.

The result of all this is a contradiction that is inherent in the policy of assimilation: it is precisely the *assimilados* (whom Portugal used as compliant assistants in domination) who question the colonizer's culture. Frustated in his aspirations, the *assimilado* tries to regain his identity, and can do so only by reverting to the masses from which he comes. Needing to identify with the subject people, the indigenous *'petite bourgeoisie'* deny that the culture of the ruling power is superior to theirs, as claimed. When the 'return to the sources' extends beyond the individual and expresses itself in 'groups' or 'movements', this opposition turns into conflict (concealed or open), the prelude to the movement of pre-independence or struggle for liberation from the foreign yoke. This 'return to the sources' is historically important only if it involves both a genuine commitment to the fight for independence and also a total, definitive identification with the aspirations of the masses, who contest not the foreigner's culture merely but foreign rule altogether. Otherwise 'return to the sources' is nothing but a means to obtaining temporary advantages, a conscious or unconscious form of political opportunism.[1]

The *assimilado* uses his privileged position to shelter the community from which he stems and to give expression to his political beliefs; once he becomes culturally conscious, he is forced, inevitably, to assume a political attitude.

Intellectual resistance

The resistance of African intellectuals in this century began between 1922 and 1933, when new movements in Angola and Mozambique

1. Cabral, op cit.

advocated the revival of African cultures—reflected in the names they gave to their newspapers: *Angolense* (The Angolan), *O Farol do Povo* (The Lighthouse of the People), *O Brado Africano* (The Cry of Africa). These movements were stopped by Lisbon. Numerous African publicists were banned or compelled to silence, and censorship was imposed on the press and on publishing in general.[1]

Not until the end of the forties did the African intellectuals find an outlet again. On the initiative of the poet Viriato da Cruz, a group of *assimilados* in Angola started the magazine *Mensagem* (The Message) in 1948. It was:[2]

> . . . dedicated to poetry in Portuguese, but it is not difficult to understand the alarm which it raised among the authorities. The poetry did not voice anything directly political; even Salazar's police could not suppose that its authors might form a kind of political party. But what they wrote, all the more touching through their poetic force, was indirectly subversive to the whole established order. In this respect, the epigraph *Vamos Descobrir Angola* (Let us Discover Angola) of the journal was in itself a radical programme, for it supposed that the 'assimilados' ought to begin to 'disassimilate', to find their way back to their African origins, to their indigenous personality. It opposed the idea of an African civilization to that of the Portuguese civilization. It implied that the former could not prosper except in the absence of the latter.

The poets described the drama of colonial suppression and exploitation, advocating the immediate emancipation of the Angolan people, if need be by force. Mário de Andarde, poet and one of the founders of the movement, attributes the reawakening of the consciousness of these intellectuals mainly to the efforts of the local publications. Viriato Cruz tries to get nearer to the people by employing their language. The message of his poetry is that the time of the black man's silence and resignation has passed, and freedom must be reconquered by revolt.[3]

A similar movement developed in Mozambique around the revived journal *O Brado* (The Cry) (the former *Brado* was banned in 1933);

1. Lemos, op. cit.
2. Davidson, op. cit., p. 152–3.
3. Lemos, op. cit., p. 5.

the poets concerned included José Craveirinha, Noémia de Sousa, Marcelino dos Santos (Kalungano) and Sérgio Vieira.

These movements not only resumed cultural claims but added a political dimension. 'The true poet has at the same time become a political pamphleteer', wrote Mário de Andrade. Stimulated by the protest movement, the *assimilado* 'will overcome the contradictions that are caused by cultural dualism' (Mário de Andrade) and use his privileged position to work for the resurrection of an authentic indigenous culture which is being preserved and continued by the mass of the people despite all the efforts of the colonizers to destroy it.

While this consciousness continued to develop in the colonies, a group of *assimilados* (Agostinho Neto, Amilcar Cabral and Mário de Andrade), studying in Lisbon, were pondering on their own culture.[1]

> *Déracinés* as they were, these men seemed to have felt vividly the gulf that separated the elite which they were and the 'masses' on the adherence of which everything would depend.

They founded the Centre for African Studies and published African poetry in Portuguese on the new protest movement and the new consciousness of an indigenous culture—a further stimulus for the nationalism which was still germinating. Andrade wrote a study of the Kumbundu language.[2]

The creation of the centre in the fifties marked the first step towards re-Africanizing minds and rejecting assimilation.[3]

> We summoned up the image of our dominated countries and so became conscious of our culture; and then came the necessity of forming political movements. It can thus be reaffirmed that, quite evidently, this re-Africanization of minds which had expressed itself in resisting assimilation had, since the end of the war, opened the way for the formation of nationalist organizations.

It may also be pointed out that the intellectuals behind the centre reappear later, at the head of the political movements in Angola, Guinea and Mozambique.

1. Davidson, op. cit., p. 156.
2. ibid.
3. Andrade, op. cit.

In the climate created by these various liberating initiatives, writers began to infiltrate the Portuguese language itself, and use it in the towns as a means of revolutionary culture. By the end of the fifties, they were modifying its structure by incorporating linguistic elements of African languages like Kumbundu. The verse of Agostinho Neto, Luandino Vieira and Alda Lara incorporates specific features of traditional Kumbundu and Umbundu poetry. In a dialectic process, the very Portuguese language that served the colonial power as an instrument of alienation was being used against it as a vehicle for ideas that preached emancipation from colonial domination.[1]

> The thread of the ancient cultures has not been broken. . . . It is the *assimilados* who will be dead to colonial culture in order to live the values of the 'indigenous' civilization.[2]

This unyielding attitude cannot very often be found in other formely colonized countries. In general they have accommodated themselves to the colonizer's culture and language without breaking with their spirit or readapting them to the new situation. Even when their own languages were respected again and they were in a position to recuperate their intellectual heritage, they have mostly not introduced any new ferment, and dynamic, native creativeness that would bring back everywhere among their people this regained culture.[3]

The impact of Portuguese colonialism thus affected cultural equilibrium, but never profoundly enough to change the traditional culture of the mass of the people. As Amilcar Cabral points out, it is not true that the independence movements were preceded by a 'cultural renaissance of the dominated people'; rather was there a revived interest sparked off by the 'return to the sources' of a small élite of *assimilados* who felt that this was the only way of establishing real contact with their own people—who had never lost their own culture.[4]

> Repressed, persecuted, betrayed by some social groups who were in league with the colonialists, African culture survived all the storms, taking refuge in the villages, in the forests

1. Gueboza and Vieira, op. cit.
2. Andrade, op. cit.
3. Lacheraf, op. cit.
4. Amilcar Cabral, 'National Liberation and Culture, 1970', Eduardo Mondlane Memorial Lecture, delivered at Syracuse University, 20 February 1970; and Cabral, op. cit.

and in the spirit of the generations who were victims of colonialism. Like the seed which long awaits conditions favourable to germination in order to assure the survival of the species and its development, the culture of African peoples flourishes again today, across the continent, in struggles for national liberation. . . . This is why the problem of a 'return to the sources' or of a 'cultural renaissance' does not put itself, nor can it put itself with respect to the popular masses: for they are the bearers of culture, they are the source of culture and, at the same time, the only entity truly capable of preserving and creating the culture, of making the history.

In the short term, Portugal had some success by creating for its own purposes an assimilated élite, alienated from its own people. In the long run, this policy becomes a victim of its inherent contradictions when the *assimilados* themselves begin, with vehemence and lucidity, to question the values of the colonial culture.

IV Information

1   Public information

The legal framework

Freedom of information was, in principle, recognized in the Portuguese colonies. Article 8.4 of the former Portuguese Constitution listed freedom of opinion and expression in any form as a part of civil rights. Since the exercise of the right of informing and of being informed cannot be separated from the exercise of political rights in general, however, and since such political rights are much restricted, the exercise of the information rights in the colonies were similarly subject to severe and fundamentally important limitations.

These limitations are incorporated in the Constitution. Article 8.2 reads:[1]

> Special laws shall regulate the exercise of the freedom of expression of thought, and the freedom of education, assembly, association and religion, which are, with regard to the first, to hinder, preventively or by repression, the perversion of the public opinion in its function as social force and to safeguard the moral integrity of the citizens.

Article 22 stated that:

> Public opinion is an essential concern of the policy and the administration of the country, the responsibility of safeguarding the country against all factors that distort truth, justice, good administration and the commonweal resting with the State.

1. This revised text of the Constitution (1971) makes a few minor changes only.

Limitation of the freedom of information is a necessity which is recognized in all democratic States, in so far as respect of the freedom of others or of established morals and customs call for such a limitation. On this general principle, various activities and discussions were forbidden in the colonies and control was imposed on everything that might be addressed to the public. As will be seen later, however, law and general practice curtailing the freedom of information were mainly inspired by the desire to cement the colonial position. 'Distorting influences' in the colonies meant any criticism of government policies and, in particular, any views that might endanger the 'integrity of the national territory' (i.e. Portugal and the colonies). To a certain degree, criticism of the way in which government policy was carried out was sometimes allowed in the press.

The basic ideas underlying the control of the mass media were explained by a leading Portuguese official in an address to the Institute of High Military Studies. The first factors to be considered were[1]

. . . the circumstances created by the subversive wars being fought overseas, which raise acute problems not only in the battle zones but also even behind the lines, i.e. in the metropolis.

In the course we have taken, our point of departure was that, in the metropolis we must immediately do everything possible to prevent anything that might hinder the defence of the values for which we are fighting in the Overseas Provinces.

To this end, we have concentrated on efficiently organizing all counteracting forces. It is not possible to list them in full, because they vary according to the tactics which the enemy, depending on circumstances, may adopt. But some of these tactics are already well known, so that the first step is to reorganize them and try to find the best method of defeating them successfully.

Subversive propaganda takes diverse forms. Sometimes, ably disguised, it is designed to calumniate or discredit the defence effort, and is aimed not only against the armed forces, but also indirectly at the population. It takes the most varied forms, from rumours to the systematic repetition of news and articles that try to stir up revulsion against the

---

1. Geraldes Cardoso, 'A Imprensa e a Informação', *Informação Cultura Popular Turismo; Gabinete Tecnica da Secretaria de Estado da Informação e Turismo*, p. 16–17 (Lisbon), No. 3, August-October 1971.

attitudes of countries that are fighting on similar fronts against the same enemies.

They do not appear to have had much success in large sectors of the population. But this does not mean that an intensive effort is not needed to protect such people against this propaganda which, in the long run, may produce a deplorable degree of confusion and corrosion if nothing is done about it.

Influence on the colonies

The influence of colonialism on information in the colonies depended on the attitude to information in Portugal itself. Everything that officially happened in the colonies was in the last instance controlled by Portugal, which supplied most of the news through Portuguese press agencies, broadcast directly to the colonies, and furnished a large proportion of the news films.

All the mass media were subject to pre-censorship. Press censorship was to be maintained as long as the 'situation of subversion' declared by the National Assembly on 20 December 1971, continued. While Article 128.1 of the Press Act stated that 'The Commission of Censorship is hereby dissolved', Article 129 reads:

> In accordance with the resolution of the National Assembly . . . the periodicals here referred to shall remain subject to pre-censorhip as long as the circumstances considered in the said resolution continue to exist.

This 'situation of subversion' was, in the words of former Prime Minister Caetano to last 'as long as the present conditions overseas continue'.[1] He justified the continuance of censorship by saying that 'for nearly half a century Portugal's daily press has been subjected to pre-censorship, and it must emerge from this gradually'.[2] Formerly, newspapers had to include a note in each issue saying that it had been submitted to the Commission of Censorship before publication. Article 101 now stated that 'in the published text or illustrations, no reference to or indication of submission to pre-censorship shall be allowed'.

1. Marcello Caetano, television address of 11 May 1972.
2. ibid.

Some critical magazines, e.g. *Seara Nova*, circumvented this by always inserting the full text of Article 101 itself.

The mass media were allocated a special role in relation to the colonies, as the following statement by a Portuguese official indicates:[1]

> We are working hard in our tent in the field. We also have our headquarters, but on both sides we are defending the same Castle, the one Fatherland that embraces several continents. . . .
>
> In diplomacy as in information—it is hard to know where one ends and the other begins—the battle is being fought with all the discipline and energy of which we are capable.
>
> What is necessary is for all these activities to be coordinated so that everybody feels himself bound to the others by the same sentiment of serving the Fatherland in which we were born.
>
> None of us is different. All are equal. Equal, when we defend the country in which we were born and hope to die; equal in the fervour of our respect for the past, dedication to the present, and hope for the future.

Portugal itself was a political dictatorship, in which people were deprived of their political rights, including their right to information. It is, therefore, hard to distinguish which measures in regard to information were a direct result of colonization, and which were due to a political situation which affected Portugal itself as much as the colonies (including, of course, the European population living in the colonies). From 1870 to 1926, when Portugal had a liberal government, the colonies enjoyed a relatively free press.[2] Some curtailing factors can unequivocally be identified as direct results of colonialism, e.g. the prohibition of any expression of opinion which calls in question the 'integrity of the national territory'; others can be traced back to the determination of an élite in power to ban any views that might prejudice the *status quo*.

Public information in operation

In the colonies, the Governor, duly authorized by the Constitution and the political considerations just mentioned, was to take measures

---

1. Ramiro Valadão, 'Problemática da Televisão', *Informação Cultura Popular Turismo*, op. cit., p. 62.
2. For this period, see Douglas L. Wheeler and René Pélissier, *Angola*, p. 84–93, New York, Washington and London, 1971.

to safeguard against what he deemed to be distorting influences. Radio stations had to be licensed, and all printed materials were pre-censored.[1]

> Since 1933 when censorship was imposed in Mozambique, writers and journalists, especially those who have attacked what they considered to be a climate of social injustice in the province, have been watched with interest by the authorities. Some have been deported; some imprisoned; some have complied with the official point of view; and others have gone into voluntary exile.

Liberty of movement was enjoyed only by those journalists 'photographic reporters, radio correspondents and film and television operators who possessed a *cartão de livre trânsito* (card allowing free movement) issued by the directors of the national information centres.[2] To prevent what might be considered as distortion of the official point of view outside of the colonies, the movements of foreign correspondents were frequently restricted. This applied in particular to northern Mozambique and north-west Angola, where—apart from the areas which Portugal no longer controlled—the liberation movements were most active.[3]

Support of government policy

In addition to the negative aspect of preventing criticism via the mass media, the State actively used them to bolster up the *status quo*.

This was made clear in the address (already mentioned) to the Institute of Higher Military Studies:[4]

> It is therefore necessary to define clearly in which sense (and to which ends) this supervision is to be exercised.
> It obviously does not simply imply a coordinating activity, more or less temporizing or passive in character, or at most the official selection and transmission of news, or even the control and supervision of information to prevent misuse.

---

1. Allison Butler Herrick *et al.*, *Area Handbook for Mozambique*, p. 127, Washington, 1969.
2. For Angola, see *Diploma Legislativo* by the Governor-General of Angola of June 1963, Articles 1 and 2.
3. Allison Butler Herrick *et al.*, op. cit., p. 178; and Allison Butler Herrick *et al.*, *Area Handbook for Angola*, p. 243, Washington, 1967.
4. *Informação Cultura Popular Turismo*, op. cit., p. 16–17.

133

Nor must it be limited to purely defensive action . . . .
i.e. to an activity which might—not altogether correctly—be
called pure counter-propaganda.

Without prejudice to any of these other purposes, what
is vital is that we should understand supervision to mean
the permanent stimulation of information, co-ordinated and
persistent, rationally planned, making use of the best information techniques, safeguarding opinion of course against
factors which mislead it, but at the same time anticipating
all efforts to do so. . . .

Therefore, all available resources must be mobilized in
order to enlighten public opinion and strengthen its convictions, creating and developing a community spirit which
will at all times constitute an insuperable barrier to the
infiltration of disruptive ideas.

The role of the Portuguese army in using the mass media for colonialist
propaganda and as a counter against nationalist aspirations is referred
to in a publication on Angola prepared by the Higher Institute
of Social Sciences and Overseas Policy:[1]

Against such propaganda . . . the Portuguese authorities
employ, as we have indicated, recognized means and
methods, and it seems useful to recall in the study which
follows that, apart from radio broadcasts and direct psychological action, subversion has been fought by means of wall
papers, placards, pamphlets etc. . . . As happened in Guinea
and in the State of India,[2] the unleashing of terrorism in
Angola took the armed forces of the metropolis there, and
these then devised and circulated various press publications
sui generis made by soldiers in war.

Newspapers and radio stations were obliged by law to give official
news as it was presented to them. Compare Article 23 of the former
Constitution:

As the press performs a public function, it may not, in
matters of national interest, refuse to insert semi-official

1. José Júlio Gonçalves, 'A Informação em Angola—Alguns Subsídios para o seu Estudo', *Angola*,
Instituto Superior de Ciências Sociais e Política Ultramarina, Curso de Extensão Universitária
Ano Lectivo de 1963–1964, Lisbon, p. 306–8.
2. Estado da India is the official name for the colonies Goa, Damão and Dio which form part
of the Republic of India since 1961 but which Portugal still officially regards as Portuguese territories occupied by a foreign power.

news items which may be sent to it by the Government. . . .
Radio and television also perform a public function. . . .

In addition to using enforceable powers, the government spent considerable amounts in winning over newsmen, e.g. $200,000 in 1962 on a public relations campaign, including an Angolan tour for fifty-six newsmen travelling under the auspices of the National Editorial Association. The aim was to give 'maximum publicity to the myth of a "Communist invasion" of Angola'.[1]

Agencies controlling information

In 1959, information and tourist centres were established in Angola and Mozambique (Centro de Informação e Turismo de Angola (CITA), and Centro de Informação e Turismo de Moçambique (CITM) under the juridiction of the governor-general and under the general supervision of the Agencia-Geral do Ultramar (General Overseas Agency) (AGU) in Lisbon. Their main purpose was to form and direct public opinion. The AGU was made responsible for co-ordinating and improving the distribution of news and preventing press and radio activities which might be interpreted as threatening peace and security. The centres were meant to (a) circulate news service items to small newspapers and radio stations; (b) act as a publishing house for government publications; and (c) control the formation of technical institutes for the training of radio and newspaper personnel. They also controlled tourist services and issued travel permits in restricted areas to local and foreign press, radio, television and cinema personnel. In Angola, CITA operated the government-owned Rádio Angola.

The centres received their information from the private (but officially controlled) Portuguese news agencies Agência Noticiária Lusitana (ANL) and Agência Nacional de Informações (ANI) as well as from the international news agencies. News from the latter was translated, summarized and passed on to subscribers.[2] As stated in the *Lei Orgânica dos Centros de Informação e Turismo* (March 1973), the control of the information centres by the AGU in Lisbon continued

1. John Marcum, *The Angolan Revolution*, Vol. I: *The Anatomy of an Explosion (1950–1962)*, p. 272. Cambridge, Mass., and London, 1969.
2. See: Allison Butler Herrick *et al.*, *Area Handbook for Angola*, op. cit., p. 243–4; and their *Area Handbook for Mozambique*, op. cit., p. 179.

despite the revision of the Constitution which was supposed to grant greater autonomy to the colonies.

Propaganda was centrally directed by AGU (which was a department of the Overseas Ministry). In 1969–70, it subsidized twenty-nine Portuguese and twenty-seven foreign newspapers and other periodicals 'in return for the insertion of articles, news items, photographs and advertisements regarding the Overseas Provinces'. It subsidized the privately owned Portuguese news agency ANL (see above).[1] It sent the centres photographs on topical events in Portugal and articles by Portuguese authors daily: 1,500 photographs and 125 articles in 1969.[2] It used radio and television, and provided the centres with blank films for making television reports. From the Lisbon radio station it started a twice-weekly programme, *Rádio Clube Português*. Copies went to the armed forces in Guinea and were broadcast locally.[3] The AGU propaganda budget in 1970 was 4.5 million escudos.[4]

The extent of both propaganda and information control varied in the colonies according to the local social and political conditions. When the situation was crucial in northern Angola at the beginning of the armed revolt in 1961, practically no news was published at all.[5] This happened as soon as a particularly serious situation arose. Public information in Guinea, where the political and military conditions were far more critical than in Angola or Mozambique, can serve as an example. Executive Order No. 2107[6] created a service for the

> . . . coordination and integration of information, civilian and military, at all levels . . . [Article 1].

> The regulations for the operation of the service shall subsequently be approved and distributed to all organizations and bureaux engaged in the gathering of intelligence [Article 2].

An Information Commission was set up and constituted as follows:

> Chairman: The Governor of the Province; Members: The Commander-in-Chief of the Armed Forces in Guinea, the

1. *Relatórios das Actividades do Ministério do Ultramar*, 1969, p. 121; and 1970, p. 250–1.
2. ibid., 1969, p. 120–1.
3. ibid., 1972, p. 252.
4. ibid., 1972, p. 261.
5. Wheeler and Pélissier, op. cit., p. 190.
6. *Boletim Oficial da Guiné*, 29 July 1969.

Commandant of the Maritime Defense of Guinea; the Independent Territorial Commandant of Guinea, the Commandant of the Air Zone of Cape Verde and Guinea, the Commandant of the Public Security Police Corps, the Chief of the Sub-Commissariat of International Police and State Defense, the Chief of the Provincial Division of the Civil Administrative Service Police; Secretary: The Chief of the Intelligence Section of the Office of the Commander-in-Chief of the Armed Forces [Article 3].

Other factors

To the legal and political factors which limited the free flow of information in the colonies, a number of others must be added. In 1966, 75 per cent of the population of Angola (and 85 per cent of that of Mozambique in 1957) were entirely dependent on oral communication for information and news.[1]

> Information among Africans was primarily transmitted by tradesmen and travellers and exchanged at public meeting places such as village markets, and by people returning from extended periods of work in other areas. In addition, persons such as missionaries, catechists and traders in contact with both towns and villages, spread information in the more remote areas.

But even this way of informing people was rendered difficult by a number of circumstances. A major obstacle was the very low population density. According to the 1970 census, population density in Angola was 4.6, in Mozambique 10.5 and in Guinea 13.5 per square kilometre (slightly above the African average of 12.0). Of the Portuguese territories in Africa, only the Cape Verde Islands, and São Tomé and Príncipe, are densely populated, with an average of 67.5 and 76.6 per square kilometre respectively.[2]

Further complications were added by the multiplicity of languages. Some 95 per cent in Angola and Mozambique speak Bantu languages, but various ethno-linguistic groups (eleven in Angola and nine in Mozambique) have great difficulty in understanding each other. These

1. Allison Butler Herrick *et al.*, *Area Handbook for Angola*, op. cit., p. 241; and their *Area Handbook for Mozambique*, op. cit., p. 177.
2. *Anuário Estatístico*, Vol. II, Instituto Nacional de Estatistica, Lisbon, 1970.

groups consist of series of 'tribes' having languages which vary. Guinea has seven ethno-linguistic groups. Cape Verde and São Tomé and Príncipe enjoy a certain linguistic uniformity: a Creole dialect based on archaic Portuguese, but modified and simplified through contact with African languages.[1]

A third factor was the poverty of transport. In Angola and Mozambique ('settlement' colonies), roads and railways mainly served to connect the industrial centres to seaports or link places of European settlement. The African population, in general, had no developed transport facilities. Guinea, until recently, had no roads, all communication being by water. The few roads meanwhile built were mainly strategic, to facilitate the movement of Portuguese soldiers

Some people working in the modern sector of the economy could make contact by radio-telephone and private radio transmitters. In 1970, 331 amateur transmitting sets were officially licensed in Angola, and 200 in Mozambique (1969).[2]

All these obstacles are material, and it is mainly Africans who were handicapped by them. The white population was not similarly dispersed, but concentrated in cities, industrial centres or places of settlement. It has a single language, Portuguese; and roads and railways which were built precisely to provide a link between such centres. Material difficulties thus exacerbate the problems of African access to information.

As we shall see, radio, press and cinemas were largely confined to urban areas and, for all practical purposes, using only Portuguese, were inaccessible to the vast majority of Africans.

1. See: D. M. Abshire and M. A. Samuels (eds.), *Portuguese Africa, A Handbook*, p. 109 ff., London and New York, 1969.
2. *Angola, Anuário Estatístico, 1970,* Luanda, and *Moçambique, Anuário Estatístico, 1969,* Lourenço Marques.

2 The press

Developments since 1961

Before the beginning of the armed revolts, the press received little attention as a factor in Portuguese colonial policy. There were two interrelated reasons: first, it was not in Portugal's interest to keep the population informed of what was going on; secondly, the influence of the press was limited because of almost total illiteracy. Guinea had its first daily newspaper (*Arauto*) only in 1947. It was not typeset, but simply duplicated. In 1954, its circulation still did not exceed 300. It was published by the Catholic Mission.[1]

With the liberation movements, the picture changed. The colonial government and white settlers recognized both the importance of being better informed, and of the potentiality of the press for propaganda purposes. This is duly noted in a publication of the Institute for Social Sciences and Overseas Policy (ISSOP).[2]

Table 19 gives details about daily newspapers and other periodicals appearing in 1970 in the Portuguese colonies in Africa. At the time of writing, Angola had ninety-four periodicals, as against thirty-one in 1961. In 1970, Guinea had no newspaper, *O Arauto* (see above), disappearing in 1964.[3] In January 1972 a daily newspaper, *A Voz da Guiné*, was launched by a priest, Cruz de Amaral, who had also been

1. Instituto Superior de Ciências Sociais e Política Ultramarina, *Cabo Verde, Guiné, São Tomé e Príncipe*, Curso de Extensão Universitária Ano Lectivo de 1965–1966, p. 202 ff, Lisbon; and *Bilan du Monde* (Belgium), Tournai, Vol. II, p. 430.
2. Instituto Superior de Ciências Sociais e Política Ultramarina, *Angola*, Curso de Extensão Universitária Ano Lectivo de 1963–1964, p. 303, Lisbon.
3. *O Arauto*, Bissau, 17 April 1964.

TABLE 19. Newspapers and other periodicals (1970)

Newspapers/periodicals	Cape Verde	Guinea	São Tomé and Príncipe	Angola	Mozambique
Total number	10	6	2	94	38
Type					
General	1	6	2	38	18
Philosophy, religion	7	—	—	3	1
Social sciences, law	2	—	—	24	4
Pure and applied sciences	—	—	—	22	11
Fine arts	—	—	—	—	—
Entertainment and sport	—	—	—	2	3
Philology, linguistics, literature	—	—	—	—	1
History, geography, biography	—	—	—	5	—
Number of copies					
Up to 500	1	—	2	5	1
501 to 900	3	3	—	5	1
901 to 1,900	—	—	—	20	8
1,901 to 7,000	3	—	—	24	4
7,001 to 15,000	—	—	—	6	5
15,001 and over	3	2	—	34	19
Frequency					
Daily	—	—	—	5	5
Three times a week	—	—	—	1	—
Twice a week	—	—	—	4	—
Weekly	3	2	2	12	7
Other	7	4	—	72	26
Price[1]					
Free	...	...	...	30	17
Up to 1 escudo	...	...	...	2	1
1.10 to 2.50 escudos	...	...	...	20	13
2.60 to 5 escudos	...	...	...	1	2
5.10 to 10 escudos	...	...	...	8	1
Over 10 escudos	...	...	...	33	6

1. For Mozambique: 1969 prices (total number of periodicals = 40).
Sources: Instituto Nacional de Estatística, *Anuário Estatístico, Províncias Ultramarinas*, Vol. II 1970; INE, *Anuário Estatístico 1970* (Angola), Delegaçao de Angola, Luanda, Mozambique; INE, *Anuário Estatístico 1969*, Delegaçao de Moçambique, Lourenço Marques.

TABLE 20. Numbers of newspapers[1] per 1,000 inhabitants

	Daily		Non-daily	
	1960	1967	1960	1967
Angola	5[2]	10	5[3]	6
Mozambique	3	7	2	5
Guinea	2	4	3	...
Africa	12[2]	11	...	...
Portugal	63	71	...	...

1. According to the Unesco definition, a newspaper of general interest issued at least four times a week is considered as a daily newspaper; one appearing three times a week or less is considered as a non-daily.
2. Figure for 1959.
3. Figure for 1958.
Source: Unesco statistical yearbooks for 1963 and for 1970.

editor of *Arauto*.[1] This was done in accordance with the detailed 14-point programme announced early in 1972.[2]

Table 20 reflects the press situation in the sixties. Despite the increase, the number of dailies per 1,000 inhabitants remained below the African average, and much below the Portuguese. In view of the high rate of illiteracy among Africans, the figure has little value as a criterion. Moreover, the dailies were published in Portuguese only. (See Table 21). The weekly *O Brado Africano*, published by the African Association of the Province of Mozambique, had one page in the Ronda language in each issue. This, however, was not very useful either, since Africans frequently cannot read the language they speak.[3]

An ISSOP book on Mozambique published in the mid-sixties confirms:[4]

> Thus, the Mozambique press is addressed in practice only to the inhabitants of the Province who read Portuguese, i.e. most of the European settlers and their families and a few literate Africans. But the great mass of the population is not

1. Radio Lisbon, 29 December 1971.
2. *Financial Times*, 5 January 1971.
3. Instituto Superior de Ciências Sociais e Política Ultramarina, *Moçambique*, Curso de Extensão Universitária Ano Lectivo de 1964–1965, p. 506, Lisbon.
4. ibid., p. 501, 503.

TABLE 21. Mozambique: periodicals according to language (1965)

| | Newspapers of general interest | | Other periodicals |
	Total	Daily	
Published in only one language			
Portuguese	10	4	23
English	—	—	1
Published in more than one language			
Portuguese and native	2	—	—
Portuguese, French and English	—	—	2

Source: *Estatísticas da Educação Ano Lectivo 1964–65*, Direcção Provincial dos Serviços de Estatística, Lourenço Marques.

reached by the numerous newspapers circulating in the Province. . . .

. . . Of over 35 periodicals in Mozambique—including at least 10 newspapers, three of wide circulation—practically all are written and published in Portuguese. Hence they are directed at some 100,000 persons only (of whom only about 25% read newspapers), whereas the six million natives have no newspaper, apart from Protestant and Mussulman periodicals or Catholic newspapers of limited circulation (*O Brado Africano* may have a few more readers than the others).

The press and the African population

The majority of the population is rural. Newspapers and periodicals were published only in the urban centres and, for lack of transport, had a reduced radius of distribution. In Mozambique, the daily *Notícias* had the highest circulation (20,000). In Guinea, the Cape Verde Islands and São Tomé and Príncipe all newspapers (except *Notícias de Cabo Verde* which was published in Mindelo) were published in the capital and had an extremely small circulation. Of the twenty-nine periodicals in Angola in the mid-sixties, seventeen (all dailies) were published in Luanda, and seven of the remaining twelve were published in towns with a comparatively large percentage of whites.[1]

By 1969, only one daily newspaper was published outside Luanda (in Lobito).[2] In Mozambique, all important periodicals, including all the dailies, were published in the capital, Lourenço Marques, or in Beira, the second centre of white settlement.

According to ISSOP, the development of such information media in Mozambique was intimately correlated with the economic and social situation of the province. Apart from the other factors mentioned, it points out that expansion depends in the first place on the development of the transport system. Air traffic was more advanced in Mozambique than in the metropolis, numerous air lines allowing the dispatch of newspapers from some centres to others, though this was generally not a daily service. But air mail is expensive and, consequently, the air transport of newspapers did not increase, since the standard of living of the population—for understandable reasons—was not at present tending to rise.

On the other hand (since it would scarcely be economic to increase the number of competing journals) surface transport was not improving rapidly enough to enlarge the area of distribution of the newspapers that already existed in the coastal cities, and reach the hinterland before the news lost all news value.[3]

The ISSOP author also touches on a vital question but does not elaborate: the capacity of people to pay for information. The very low level of rural wages has already been described. In 1971, the minimum daily wages (in escudos) of rural workers in Mozambique were fifteen in the northern, nineteen in the middle, and twenty-two in the southern districts. Of these, up to 50 per cent could be legally deducted by the employer for food, clothing and housing, leaving, in the worst case, 8 escudos ($U.S.0.25 to $U.S.0.30) a day.[4] The population was predominantly rural. If, as is realistic, we assume that most employers do not voluntarily pay more than the minimum wage, it is easy to imagine how much an African could in these circumstances afford to spend on newspapers, most of which cost 1.10 to 2.5 escudos (see Table 19), i.e. about a third of their available daily money. The

1. Centro de Informaçaõ e Turismo de Angola, *Jornalismo de Angola*, Luanda, 1964.
2. Agência-Geral do Ultramar, Centro de Informaçaõ e Turismo de Angola, *Norberto Gonzaga, Angola, Pequena Monografia*, Lisbon, 1969.
3. Instituto Superior de Ciências Sociais e Politica Ultramarina, *Moçambique*, op. cit., p. 506, 508.
4. Joachim F. Kahl, *Pro und kontra Portugal. Der Konflikt um Angola und Mosambik*, p. 141, Stuttgart, 1972.

most popular dailies, *A Província de Angola* and *Notícias* in Mozambique, cost 2.50 and 2 escudos respectively.

Contents

The question of content is perhaps even more important than the question of price.

Apart from newspapers, there were cultural, technical, economic and administrative periodicals and bulletins. The *Revista de Angola* was of general interest. Most publications had a circulation of less than 2,000 per issue.

Newspapers published local and Portuguese news, and official notices. Foreign news was covered only by the dailies, and frequently treated in 'human angle' terms. Local news coverage tended to be limited to the place of publication, except in the case of *A Província de Angola* and *Notícias* (Mozambique) which also devoted a large proportion of their space (50 per cent and 75 per cent respectively) to advertisements and sport. Portugal received conspicuous treatment, from long reports about the weather to leading articles on the cost of taxis in Lisbon. Most of the news concerned the speeches and travel of ministers, and opinions regarding matters in the African provinces.

The press did not publish criticism of Portuguese policy in the colonies although it may occasionally have criticized certain aspects of its implementation. In the last electoral campaign, during Caetano's office not a single newspaper in Angola gave the opposition's views on the overseas problem. The press in Mozambique ran a campaign to discredit the opposition.[1] The only exception was the *Voz de Moçambique*, published by the Associação dos Naturais de Moçambique (mainly Europeans or mulattos born in the colonies). This paper maintained a certain independence and openly expressed the interests of the African population.[2]

It must, of course, be remembered that newspapers were subject to pre-censorship, but it is not this that essentially determined their editorial policy. The press in the colonies served the interests both of colonial policy and of the settlers. The fact that the interests of the settlers do not always coincide with those of Lisbon partly explains

1. United Nations document A/8023/Add.3 of 5 October 1970.
2. *Portuguese Africa*, op. cit., p. 153.

critical viewpoints occasionally expressed. Support for these two interests was voluntary and had nothing to do with pre-censorship (as can be deduced from the continuous 'patriotic' statements made by the newspapers on their own initiative).

A splendid example of the identification of the press with colonial policy is afforded by Guinea. As mentioned above, a priest, Cruz de Amaral, was editor and director of *A Voz da Guiné*, the only daily; in January 1972, the Governor of Guinea appointed him President of the Commission of Censorship.[1]

But the congruence of interests did not exist only at this level. An advertisement that appeared in *A Província de Angola* is symptomatic. A Portuguese soldier in battledress gleefully says of his enormous tin of insecticide: 'the latest—it kills till it gluts'. The association of ideas is obvious: 'terrorists' should be destroyed with as little compunction as verminous insects.

Ownership and control of newspapers

A glance at Table 22 reveals that, in 1967, 32 per cent of periodicals (including one of the largest newspapers) were government owned. The three publications owned by the Church included the important daily *Diário* (circulation 10,000 in Lourenço Marques). The Church's

TABLE 22. Press ownership, Mozambique (1967)

Ownership	Total	Number of copies					Frequency	
		up to 1,900	1,901- 7,000	7,001- 15,000	15,001- 70,000	70,001 upwards	Daily	Other
State and State institutions	11	3	3	1	3	1	—	11
Church institutions	3	—	—	—	2	1	1	2
Private companies	8	—	1	1	1	5	3	5
Private firms	1	—	—	—	—	1	—	1
Other	13	3	2	3	2	3	1	12
TOTAL	36	6	6	5	8	11	5	31

Source: Estatística da Educaçao Ano Lectivo 1966–67, Direcção Provincial dos Serviços de Estatística, Lourenço Marques.

1. *A Capital*, Lisbon, 25 January 1972.

role in information was clearly expressed in a letter in ten theses sent by the Bishop of Lourenço Marques to all his priests:[1]

> ... 7. It is the duty of native Africans to thank the colonizers for having received from them so many blessings. It is the duty of educated people to enlighten those with little education regarding the illusions of independence.

The National Overseas Bank (Banco Nacional Ultramarino) owned the *Tribuna* of Beira, exclusively controlled *Notícias*, and shared the control of *Notícias da Beira* with the Portuguese millionaire Champalimaud. *Notícias da Beira* was directed by Jorge Jardim who is said to be the leader of a movement favouring Mozambique independence along the lines of the Unilateral Declaration of Independence of Southern Rhodesia (UDI).[2] It was his newspaper which in 1971 denounced as traitors the four Catholic priests who revealed the massacres of the Portuguese army in Tete.[3] In March 1971 *Notícias da Beira* merged with the *Diário de Moçambique*.[4]

In addition to direct control the National Overseas Bank also exercised a significant editorial influence because it was the main source of loans in Mozambique. It attempted, for example, to halt publication of *A Voz de Moçambique* which—as we have seen—was the only paper to maintain a certain independence.[5]

> Early in 1965, the President of the *Associação dos Naturais de Moçambique*, who was also a member of the Mozambique Legislative Council, published a photograph of the *Banco Nacional Ultramarino* in Lourenço Marques, in *A Voz de Moçambique* with a caption quoting Winston Churchill: 'Never did so many owe so much to so few'. He was immediately fired from his job in a company that depended on the Bank for its finances, and the newspaper *Notícias*, owned by the Bank, refused to print *A Voz de Moçambique* on its presses. Several months later, he was still unemployed.

A Voz de Moçambique was forced to suspend publication for a couple of weeks, until other printing arrangements were made.

1. *Der totalitäre Gottesstaat*, ed. Michael Raske *et al.* on behalf of the *Arbeitsgemeinschaft von Priestergruppen in der BRD*, Düsseldorf 1970, p. 174.
2. United Nations document A/8023/Add.3 of 5 October 1970.
3. *Le Monde Diplomatique*, July 1972.
4. Summary of World Broadcasts, 4 March 1971.
5. *Portuguese Africa*, op. cit., p. 156.

The ISSOP points out in its book on Mozambique that some journals did not succeed in expanding, reaching a greater audience, and winning a significantly larger number of readers. They found themselves obliged to accept absorption by agencies who turned from their prime function of granting credits to the exercise of other functions. This led to a phenomenon of transfer and microconcentration, and social communications passed from the hands of those who exercise social power (intellectuals) to those who wield economic power.[1]

The picture was similar in the other colonies, none of which, however, had any single institution which concentrates as much power as the National Overseas Bank in Mozambique. São Tomé had three periodicals; one belonged to the Acçao Nacional Popular (the former government party), the other two to the Church.[2]

The propaganda press of the Portuguese army

Propaganda for the Portuguese colonial policy was one of the main purposes of the field newspapers (*jornais de campanha*) and bush newspapers (*jornais do mato*) published by the Portuguese armed forces stationed in the colonies. There were a great number of these publications, mostly addressed primarily to the soldiers, but also distributed to some extent among the population (*em circuito aberto*), e.g. *A Caserna* in Mozambique. This had twelve pages and appeared twice a month. This type of paper was short-lived, but whenever one ceased, there was always a new one to take its place. They frequently amounted to little more than pamphlets, their only purpose being to put their message across.

> . . . the armed forces have special means of information, propaganda and counter-propaganda of which it is not necessary to speak here. Let us only say, in short, that besides other means of spontaneous internal communication, some units and the command posts use leaflets, wall papers and placards to provide information or for purposes of education or counter-propaganda.[3]

Pamphlets other than those used to impart public information were published in the African languages.

1. Instituto Superior de Ciências Sociais e Política Ultramarina, *Moçambique*, op. cit., p. 508.
2. *São Tomé e Príncipe, petite monographie*, p. 120, Agência-Geral do Ultramar, Lisbon, 1970.
3. Instituto Superior de Ciências Sociais e Política Ultramarina, *Cabo Verde . . .*, op. cit., p. 246.

The main idea behind this propaganda can be inferred from a look at some of these pamphlets. One showed black and white hands greeting each other before a Portuguese flag. The text reads *Juntos venceremos* (Together we shall be victorious). The newspaper *Sempre em Frente* (Always Forward) showed the kind of victory colonial Portugal had in mind. On the front page of the newspaper was a *Monumento ao Esforço da Raça* (Monument to the race's effort). It was situated in Guinea-Bissau and glorified the Portuguese. The 'partnership' suggested in the shaking of hands as shown in the illustration could hardly be expected to overshadow the realities of Portuguese colonial policy.

For the purpose of directly fighting the support which the liberation movements were being given by the people, illustrated pamphlets written in Creole were distributed among the population. These requested Africans to leave the bush and report to the Portuguese army:

> People of the Bush. Report to the Authorities. Only deceived people live in the bush. Straight thinking people live in the village. In the bush, there is hunger, illness, and death. In the village, there is cheerfulness, there is food and there is the visit by the doctor. Come and report to the Army.

The role of the press in the colonies, accordingly, was to further colonial policy and the interests of white settlers. This almost automatically meant that it not only did not serve African interests, but was actively used against them.

3 Radio and television

Broadcasting policy from 1961 until the present Portuguese Government took power

In countries with a high rate of illiteracy, radio provides a major channel of public communication, particularly if distances are large and other communications are little developed. Prior to the sixties, the broadcasting network in the Portuguese colonies was very limited. No radio station could be received regularly throughout either Angola or Mozambique. Guinea's first station (IKW) started in 1944, and broadcast daily for only one hour, raised to two in the fifties.[1]

As programmes were in Portuguese only, most Africans had no access to them.[2]

Once fighting started, however, the Portuguese colonial government realized the value of radio for propaganda purposes and for countering broadcasts from the liberation movements. The new policy can be illustrated by the example of Angola. In March 1961, i.e. one month after the beginning of the armed revolt, a co-ordinating commission (Comissão Coordenadora do Plano de Radiodifusão da Província de Angola) was set up to 'strengthen Portugal's information policy'[3] by providing country-wide coverage from government-operated Radio Angola. The purpose and reasons were explained as follows:[4]

1. Instituto Superior de Ciências Sociais e Política Utramandora, *Cabo Verde* . . ., op. cit., p. 266 ff.
2. For Angola, see: Instituto Superior de Ciências Sociais e Política Ultramarina, *Angola*, op. cit., p. 325.
3. ibid., p. 329.
4. *Notícias*, Lourenço Marques, 30 May 1961.

Because of its instantaneous impact, radio is at present a most valuable element which, through its psychological effects, can fortify, and properly enlighten and inform.

Indeed, a service providing frequent and abundant information represents the best weapon for destroying rumours and false reports. Everyone knows of the broadcasts of various origins which fill our receivers at all hours in order to undermine public opinion; they are resolved to foster distrust and spread intrigue and misery in a truly subversive psychological campaign. We must face the enemy on all fronts with the same weapons at his own game; hence the need for the Government to recognize the urgency of improving and coordinating radio overseas, and especially in Angola. . . .

It can confidently be expected that, with the provision of financial and adequate technical means proposed, Radio Angola, properly integrated in the national broadcasting system, will contribute effectively to the solution of the problems that disturb us and threaten the integrity of the Nation, and that it will play in future the role which becomes it in the life of the Nation.

The proposed expansion was largely based on existing private stations:[1]

The project is based on using the existing infrastructure provided by the radio clubs (whose helpful and disinterested attitude cannot be over-emphasized), and on the proper coordination and wide extension of the information services.

State interference in private information services was referred to as follows in the ISSOP book on Angola:[2]

The official intervention in private information must be discreet and, if possible, indirect, in order to avoid negative results. And in areas where there are conflicts such as those we are facing in Angola, prudence and secrecy are still more necessary in handling information problems.

1. *Noticias*, Laurenço Marques, 30 May 1961.
2. Instituto Superior de Ciências Sociais e Política Ultramarina, *Angola*, op. cit., p. 329.

TABLE 23. Power of transmitters

Country and year	Under 0.999 kW	1 to 4.999 kW	5 kW and over
Angola			
1958	11	12	1
1968	9	34	5
1969	19	31	9
1970	19	31	9
Cape Verde			
1958	1	1	1
1968	2	1	1
1969	2	1	1
1970	2	1	1
Guinea			
1958	—	1	—
1968	1	—	1
1969	1	—	1
1970	1	—	1
Mozambique			
1958	3	—	1
1968	...	...	...
1969	20	1	22
1970	...	...	...
São Tomé and Príncipe			
1958	...	...	...
1968	—	1	1
1969	—	1	1
1970	1	1	1

Source: Anuário Estatístico do Ultramar 1958, Instituto Nacional de Estatística, Lisbon; *Anuários Estatísticos*, Vol. II: *Províncias Ultramarinas, 1968, 1969* and *1970*, Instituto Nacional de Estatística, Lisbon.

The expansion of radio coverage did not in fact take place until 1963, when the Defence and Overseas Ministries passed the responsibility for information policy on to the Governor-General and Commander-in-Chief of the armed forces.[1] Until 1964, no single station could be heard regularly throughout the country; Radio Angola—the only station with a transmitter of up to 10 kW—could be heard at least intermittently in most areas. By February 1964, Radio Angola had

1. *Diário do Governo de 19.2.1963.*

4 transmitters of 10 kW each. It was again expanded in 1966, to operate on six frequencies of 10 kW each and one of 3 kW.[1]

Radio stations

In 1970, 59 transmitters were operating in Angola for 2,439 hours weekly (as against 36 and 688 respectively in 1960) (see Table 24). Radio Angola had the largest audience. The leading private station was Radio Clube de Angola. The transmitter of the diamond mining company Diamang and the Companhia Angolana de Agricultura (CADA) had an anti-guerrilla role which was 'of tactical importance for the Government in combating possible infiltration'.[2] The establishment of a regional transmitter at Pereira d'Eça, capital of the recently created district of Cunene where Angola's most comprehensive irrigation and settlement project is being carried out, was announced in 1972.[3]

In Mozambique, all radio stations were privately owned and depended on commercial advertising and government subsidies (so did all privately owned stations in Angola). The most important station was Radio Clube de Moçambique (RCM), which served as an unofficial agency of the government.[4] It was the only station which could be heard throughout Mozambique, and accounted for about half of all broadcasting time. It operated a central station in Lourenço Marques and three regional stations at Nampula, Porto Amélia and Quelimane, bordering the areas where FRELIMO military activity was strongest. The regional stations broadcast in Portuguese. They also broadcasted a programme called *Voice of Mozambique* (produced by the Centro de Informação et Turismo de Moçambique (CITM)) in different African languages (Shangana and Ronga):[5]

> . . . to counter the possible effects of subversive broadcasts emanating from neighbouring States and to promote among Africans a sense of identification with the Portuguese.

As already mentioned, Guinea remained practically without radio until the end of the sixties—a fact deplored by a member of ISSOP:[6]

---

1. Allison Butler Herrick *et al.*, *Area Handbook for Angola*, op. cit., p. 253.
2. *Portuguese Africa*, op. cit., p. 308.
3. *Diário*, Angola, 8 February 1972.
4. Allison Butler Herrick *et al.*, *Area Handbook for Mozambique*, op. cit., p. 183.
5. ibid.
6. Instituto Superior de Ciências Socias e Politica Ultramarina, *Cabo verde . . .*, op. cit., p. 285.

TABLE 24. Radio stations and sets in the colonies and in Portugal

Country and year	Number of broadcasting stations		Number of transmitters	Total power of transmitters in kW	Broadcasting hours per week		Number of licensed radio sets (thousands)	Number of radios per 1,000 inhabitants
	Total	State			Total	State		
Angola								
1960	18	1	36	35	688[1]	63	53.0	11
1968	17	1	48	88	1,595	181	79.4	17
1969	18	1	59	88	1,809	121	81.6	15[2]
1970	19	1	59	480	2,439	191	84.5	15[3]
Cape Verde								
1960	3	—	3	6[4]	35[4]	—	1.8	9
1968	4	—	4	7[4]	84	—	4.4	18
1969	4	—	4	...	61	...	8.5	18
1970	4	—	4	...	79	...	8.7	...
Guinea								
1960	1	1	1	...	...	...	1.8	3
1968	1	1	2	11	13	13	3.5	7
1969	1	1	2	11	13	13	3.7	...
1970	1	1	2	...	126	126	4.0	8[3]
Mozambique								
1960	7	—	19	192	800[4]	—	37.0	6
1968	7	—	41	300[5]	804	—	89.8	12
1969	7	—	43	...	917	—	110.5	...
1970	7	—	43	...	917	—	125.7	15[3]
São Tomé and Príncipe								
1960	1	—	1	1	...	—	0.9	14
1968	1	—	2	6	68	—	2.6	...
1969	1	—	2	6	68	—	2.1	...
1970	1	1	3	...	163	163	...	...
Portugal								
1960[6]	...	1	62	1,732	...	—	848.0	95
1968	57	1	106	...	...	366	1,397.0	147
1969	67	1	142	...	...	380	1,405.6	...
1970	73	1	151	...	...	...	1,405.1	163

1. *Anuário Estatístico de Angola 1960* (author's calculations).
2. Author's calculation on basis of population estimate by Unesco.
3. Author's calculation on basis of provisional data of 1970 census.
4. Estimated.
5. 1967 figure.
6. 1961 figure.
Source: Angola, *Anuários Estatísticos*, 1960 and 1970; Mozambique, *Anuários Estatísticos*, 1968 and 1969; *Anuários Estatísticos*, INE, Vols. I and II: 1968–70; *Unesco Statistical Yearbook*, 1963 and 1970; Instituto Superior de Ciências Sociais e Política Ultramarina, *Cabo Verde . . . ,* op. cit.

Under these conditions it is incapable of informing, instructing, entertaining and educating the local audience, nor can it provide in the peripheral regions the counter-propaganda that seems necessary to those who are better acquainted with these problems.

In view of the positive and growing successes of the Guinean liberation movement Partido Africano para a Independência da Guiné e Cabo Verde (PAIGC), the government was forced to expand its propaganda effort and impose a severer control on the news. In July 1969, the Office of the Commander-in-Chief took over responsibility for the co-ordination and control of information (see above). Shortly before the regional station of Guinea was integrated into the National Broadcasting System (Emissora Nacional de Radiodifusão) which provided 'all the broadcasting services necessary to satisfy the needs of the Province and to protect and defend the national interests' (Decree No. 49,084, 26 June 1969). Article 12.3 of this decree reads:

> With respect of news broadcasts and all programmes of an informative or educational nature, the Administrator shall receive direct guidance from the Governor of the Province, who may utilize the regional broadcasting station for the efficient fulfilment of his duties.

The number of hours of transmission per week in Guinea rose from 13 in 1969 to 126 in 1970 (see Table 24).

As Portugal lost control of the colony because of the activities of PAIGC, government and army multiplied their efforts. Thus in 1972, the Governor announced a new economic and social development programme which included the installation of a new radio transmitter which was to be the most powerful in western Africa.[1]

Receivers

To ensure that its propaganda could be heard, the government initiated a selective purchase-tax policy which favoured sets that receive only medium waves i.e. did not receive the short-wave programmes of the liberation movements and other hostile foreign broadcasts.[2] Apart from the annual licence fee, purchase tax on

1. *Financial Times*, 5 January 1972.
2. Kahl, op. cit., p. 157.

medium-wave sets in Mozambique at the end of the sixties varied from a minimum of 20 escudos to 1,000 escudos, while the minimum tax on short-wave receivers was ten times as much.[1]

The number of receivers per 1,000 habitants was small (see Table 24), far below the African average (which was 45 in 1969).[2] For comparison, the number of sets *per capita* in Portugal is also given. However, the real number of receivers in the colonies was considerably larger, as transistor radios in particular were not registered in order to avoid taxes and licence fees.

What is important is that these receivers were mainly concentrated in the centres of European settlement. Thus, of 125,000 receivers in Mozambique in 1969, some 55,000 were in Lourenço Marques; while of 84,000 receivers in Angola in 1970, 38,000 were registered in Luanda.[3] According to a study made in Angola in the mid-sixties, most of the sets in Angola were owned by Europeans.[4]

Language employed

Unless specifically propaganda, for example the *Voice of Mozambique*, programmes consisted mostly of information and popular music (usually European). In Mozambique in 1971, advertising and music took 86.6 per cent of the total; in 1964–65, the corresponding figure was 91.6 per cent. Cultural features occupied 1.2 per cent in 1971 (Table 25).

A picture of regular broadcasts that were not exclusively propaganda can be formed from the following (these samples do not indicate that radio was doing much to reduce the exceptionally high rates of illiteracy in the Portuguese colonies):

> Guinea: standard radio programmes, September-October 1965.[5]
>
> *Mondays*
>
> Period I
> 12.00   Opening

---

1. Allison Butler Herrick *et al.*, *Area Handbook for Mozambique*, op. cit., p. 182–3.
2. *Unesco Statistical Yearbook, 1970.*
3. *Moçambique. Anuário Estatístico 1969*, Lourenço Marques, and *Angola, Anuário Estatístico 1970*, Luanda.
4. Allison Butler Herrick *et al.*, *Area Handbook for Angola*, op. cit., p. 250.
5. Instituto Superior de Ciências Sociais e Política Ultramarina, *Cabo Verde . . .* , op. cit., p. 269.

12.05	Tangos
12.15	Echoes of the Province
12.30	Request programme (music requested by listeners)
13.00	Time signal. News
13.15	*Serão para trabalhadores* (entertainment for workers)
14.00	Interruption of transmission

Period II

18.00	Reopening
18.05	Portuguese music
18.15	Echoes of the Province
18.30	Feuilleton (romances or sentimental plays)
19.00	News
19.15	Programme of the Armed Forces
19.45	Some minutes with . . .
20.00	Time signal. Dinner concert
20.30	News
20.45	Orchestra
21.00	Rainbow (musical medley)
21.30	Music from Brazil
21.45	Sings
22.15	Let's dance
22.45	Summary of the news. Last news edition
22.55	Good-night
23.00	End of transmission

Radio Clube de Moçambique: Programme A. 21 February 1973.[1]

05.56	The Word of God (reading from the Bible)
06.00	Opening
06.05	Music
06.30	Programme 'Tic-Tac' of Elmo-Productions (commercial advertising)
07.00	News
07.10	Programme 'Tic-Tac' continued
08.30	Music
09.00	News
09.05	Wave of the Morning (Tam-Tam commercial advertising)

1. *Notícias*, Lourenço Marques, 21 February 1973.

10.00	It is still good-morning (Delta commercial advertising)
11.00	News
11.05	Rain of Stars, by Maria Helena Bramão
11.35	Variety (music and entertainment)
12.00	Music
12.30	Sound journal (first transmission)
13.00	Music
13.10	Musical groups, bands,
13.30	Film music
14.00	Portuguese songs
14.30	Music
15.00	News
15.10	Sweet Home—Programme for the housewives
16.10	Latitude 26 (Rainbow commercial advertising)
17.00	News
17.05	Latitute 26 continued
17.35	Music and songs
18.00	Portuguese programme
18.30	The day's programmes
18.40	Variety (music and entertainment)
19.00	Music
19.30	Sound journal (second transmission)
20.10	Music for dinner
20.40	Lisbon 73—RCM programme from Lisbon
21.00	Music and songs
22.00	News
22.05	Symphony 22, by Golo Productions
23.00	Portuguese songs
23.30	Music and songs
00.01	News
00.05	Listen today
00.06	Good-night
00.10	End of transmission

Language is not specifically indicated except for Mozambique (see Table 26). The percentages do not appear to differ very much in the other colonies.[1] Broadcasts in Portuguese rose from 67.9 per cent in 1966–67 to 79.9 per cent in 1972 (second quarter). This again ignores the problem of illiterates, apart from the fact that an over-

1. For Angola, see: Instituto Superior de Ciências Socias e Política Ultramarina, *Angola*, op. cit., p. 327.

TABLE 25. Mozambique: programme contents (percentage of total hours of transmission)

Type of programme	1964–65	1966–67	1968	1969	1970	1971
Information and sports	5.4	8.9	9.6	9.6	10.5	11.2
Cultural (lectures, plays, talks, literature)[1]	1.9	1.3	1.4	1.2	1.3	1.2
Theatre	1.1	1.1	0.9	1.1	1.1	1.0
Music	25.0	27.9	31.3	30.8	30.6	30.6
Advertising and other[2]	66.6	60.8	56.8	57.3	56.5	56.0

1. In 1964–65 this heading included cultural and religious features and educational broadcasting.
2. In 1964–65 the breakdown was: advertising, 63.2 per cent; other, 3.4 per cent.
Source: Calculated by the author on the basis of *Estatísticas da Educaçao Anos Lectivos 1964–65 and 1966–67*, Direcção Provincial dos Serviços de Estatística, Lourenço Marques; *Moçambique. Anuários Estatísticos*, 1968 and 1969, Instituto Nacional de Estatística, Delegação de Moçambique, Lourenço Marques *Bóletins Mensais de Estatística* 1970 and 1971, INE, Delegaçao de Moçambique, Lourenço Marques.

whelming majority of the population does not understand Portuguese. Only a very small percentage of broadcasts were transmitted in African languages (referred to as 'native languages' in the statistics). Before the beginning of the armed revolt, broadcasts were exclusively in Portuguese. The subsequent creation of programmes in African languages recognized the necessity of putting propaganda across in a language Africans understood.

TABLE 26. Mozambique: languages used (percentage of total hours of transmission)

Language	1966–67	1968	1969	1970	1971	1972[1]
Portuguese	67.9	68.9	72.7	71.7	76.5	79.9
English and Afrikaans[2]	20.3	17.8	14.5	14.8	14.8	13.1
Native languages	11.8	13.3	12.8	13.5	11.1	7.0

1. Second quarter.
2. Before 1968: English only.
Source: *Moçambique. Anuários Estatísticos* 1968 and 1969, Instituto Nacional de Estatística, Delegaçao de Moçambique, Lourenço Marques; *Estatística de Educaçao Ano Lectivo 1966-67*; Direcção Provincial dos Serviços de Estatística, Lourenço Marques; *Boletins Mensais de Estatística* 1970, 1971 and July 1972, INE, Delegaçao de Moçambique, Lourenço Marques.

The tone of these programmes in African languages can be gauged from a document of the Service for Psycho-Social Action (Serviço de Acção Psicossocial) which was responsible for the *Hora Nativa*, an RCM programme for Africans. The document reads:[1]

> The simple fact that our advice and suggestions are being transmitted by an authoritative voice that contacts the peoples in their own language is for the more retarded a guarantee of authenticity, omniscience and infallibility. As he who has been taught to read [*alfabeto*] piously believes in the printed letter, the native believes in the voice that speaks to him in his language over the air. . . .

> In social matters, we try to improve the condition of women; combat pernicious preconceptions; attentively observe the feelings of the populations, their state of mind, emotional temperature, and elements which may indicate when and how the masses can be led away from ideas of civil indiscipline; and we seek ways of counteracting disruptive theories, and captious propaganda from outside and inside.

Of Portuguese language lessons incorporated in the programme, the document states:

> To instil the desire to learn Portuguese so that they will speak of it as 'our language' is our permanent concern. The language, without any doubt, is one of the most arid fields to cultivate. Even taking the greatest care, it is hard not to saturate the audience who, failing to understand, find the programmes boring and simply switch to other stations they find more attractive.

Broadcasts from Portugal itself

The importance of broadcasts transmitted directly to the colonies was underlined in the preamble to the basic radio legislation (Decree 41,484 of 30 December 1957):

> . . . In all modern countries the radio is, with the press,

---

1. Província de Moçambique, Serviço de Acçao Psicossocial, *Breve Comentário Seguido de Algumas Cartas dos Radiouvintes Recolhidas ao acaso da Volumosa Correspondência Arquivada na Divisão de Accão Educativa e Cultural*, Lourenço Marques, March 1962.

one of the most powerful means of our times for spreading culture, imparting information, and even influencing foreign countries. Its importance cannot be overlooked, particularly when, as in our case, the different parts of the national territory are spread over various continents.

Under Article 2.1 it was accordingly a duty

... to ensure the transmission of broadcast programmes to Portuguese territories and to foreign countries in which substantial groups of Portuguese live.

The most important overseas broadcasts were transmitted from S. Gabriel (in Pegões, east of Lisbon) which had seven 100-kW short-wave transmitters and twenty-three directed antennae.[1] These transmitters covered all areas where Portugal possessed colonies, from the Cape Verde Islands to Timor and including the former colony of Goa, as well as those non-European areas with relatively great numbers of emigrants, for example Brazil and the west coast of the United States.

Short-wave transmission, which has many shortcomings, limited the affect of these broadcasts. Moreover, programmes were often reworded and sent to the Interchange Services (Serviços de Intercambio), but there was no guarantee that they would actually be transmitted. Efficiency was improved under the decrees passed in 1969 making the broadcasting service in Lisbon responsible for broadcasting in Guinea and in São Tomé and Príncipe.

For sixteen hours each day short-wave broadcasts were beamed to the colonies. Apart from information, the programmes were: *Meeting with Overseas*, and *Ideas and Facts* (political); *Sentimental Guide* (regional); *History of Africa* (cultural); *ABC of Portugal* (ethnographical and tourist); *Saudade* (Homesickness) (for families of military personnel overseas and crews of fishing fleets); *Lusiade Friendship Club* (for Portuguese centres in foreign countries); *Letters from Listeners* (a one-hour weekly programme started in the fifties, extraordinary rise in popularity after 1961 as troops began to be sent regularly overseas).[2]

Apart from these direct broadcasts, the Interchange Services fed

1. *Informaçao Cultura Popular Turismo*, op. cit., p. 31.
2. ibid., p. 34.

a large part of the regional stations on the Azores and in São Tomé and Príncipe, and dispatched a variety of programmes to the twenty-nine radio stations in the colonies.[1]

The broadcasts beamed from Portugal could hardly be regarded as contributing to cultural life, as they were almost exclusively propagandist. Their intensification during the last few years of Caetano's rule can be traced back to the necessity of countering nationalist aspirations. Compare the talk given by a senior official responsible for information to the Institute for Higher Military Studies:[2]

> In these conditions, in which there is neither front nor rearguard, we must without any doubt fight decisive information and counter-information battles in which audio-visual media will be decisive weapons.
>
> To be successful, we must think the structure of our telecommunications anew, realizing that, in the electronics era which has already begun, we have the means at our disposal to overcome the territorial discontinuity in which we live and, finally, to be the one single and indivisible Nation we desire. . . . Radio broadcasting can break down walls; it is a striking and penetrating force which opens the way for its own message. Expected and wanted books, newspapers, cinemas may well be, but none of them can as fully take possession as the broadcast, which intrudes into the intimacy of the home with a total absence of secrecy or tact. It grabs the defenceless listener before he has the will, time or opportunity to prepare himself to listen. It annihilates silence and privacy without compunction. It finds its way into unprotected, indifferent and absent-minded minds.

Television

There is no regular television service in the colonies. In Angola, the first occasional transmissions were made in December 1972.[3]

Mozambique hoped to have a station in Lourenço Marques early in 1973 to take programmes via satellite from Eurovision and the United States. The station was to be completed in 1974. Costing

---

1. *Informacao Cultura Popular Turismo*, op. cit., p. 36.
2. ibid., p. 41, 27.
3. *Portugal Report*, Bonn, Portuguese Embassy in the Federal Republic of Germany, February 1973.

70 million escudos, it was the first of three projected television stations (the other two being Lisbon and Luanda).[1] Another project was announced by the Commander-in-Chief of Mozambique. As part of the ambitions Operation Frontier plan to bring 'social and economic progress' to the border population in Nangade in northern Mozambique, plans for setting up a television network have been completed by army electronic engineers; the Nangade television station is expected to be in operation soon.[2]

1. *Província de Angola*, 4 March 1973.
2. *Agence France Presse*, 24 October 1972.

4 Cinema

Cinema provides the most popular form of entertainment in the colonies, and accounts for practically all public entertainment performances (see Table 27). However, despite a rapid development during the sixties, the number of cinemas was generally below the African average (without however counting the large number of mobile cinemas for which no statistical data are available). In 1967 the average cinema seating capacity in Africa was 5 per 1,000 inhabitants. This average figure was not reached in Angola until 1970. For Mozambique the figure was 2 per 1,000 inhabitants, in Guinea, 1.3 (1967).[1] Attendance was also very low: in Angola 0.5 visits annually per inhabitant in 1970; Guinea, 0.4 (1967).[2]

Again, real figures of attendance by Africans are still lower, as most cinemas are in towns (i.e. in centres of European settlement). In 1968 over 60 per cent of showings in Mozambique took place in Lourenço Marques, Beira and other urban areas. Average attendance per show: 327 in Lourenço Marques, 280 in Beira, 265 in Mozambique as a whole.[3] In July 1972, 50 per cent of showings were in Luanda. Average attendance per show in Luanda: 342; average for Angola as a whole, 252.[4]

Until 1961, most Africans were hindered by the legal discrimination which divided them into *cidadãos* (citizens) and *indígenas* (natives). Immediately after the outbreak of the armed revolt, this discrimination formally disappeared when the *Estatuto Indígena* was abolished by decree, but in many instances it still continued. Moreover, the

1. Kahl, op. cit., p. 158 and *Unesco Statistical Yearbook 1970*.
2. ibid.
3. *Moçambique. Anuário Estatístico 1963*, Lourenço Marques.
4. *Angola. Boletim Mensal de Estatística*, July 1972, Luanda.

TABLE 27. Public entertainment (1970)

	Cape Verde	Guinea	São Tomé and Príncipe	Angola	Mozambique
Buildings	6	5	1	36	28
Seating capacity	2,763	2,014	1,010	29,097	19,527
All shows	1,785	1,132	365	11,078	12,040
Cinema shows only	1,781	1,132	358	10,644	11,933
Total attendance	321,000	355,000	99,000	3,203,000	3,253,000
Cinema only	319,000	355,000	96,000	3,079,000	3,197,000
Revenue (thousands of escudos)	2,386	4,912	1,007	64,703	68,644

Source: Anuário Estatístico, Vol. II, 1970, Instituto Nacional de Estatística, Lisbon.

Africans' wages were in general so low the cinema ticket might cost him three times what he earned during the day (20 escudos in Angola, 21 in Mozambique, 14 escudos in Guinea (1970)) (compare comments by a member of the Institute for Overseas Studies).[1] Censorship was exercised by the Comissão Provincial de Exame e Classificação de Espectáculos. Politically sensitive films were unlikely to be released at all; others were censored primarily for moral content, and many were cut.[2] Figures (for Angola only) are given in Table 28.

TABLE 28. Length and type of films shown in Angola

Year	Long films (over 1,800 m)		Shorter films (up to 1,800 m)				
	Recreative	Documentary	Recreative	Documentary	Cultural	Topical	Advertising
1962	3,324	487	1,944	2,404	982	1,149	803
1966	8,011	83	3,513	4,990	1,631	3,069	3,772
1970	8,526	107	4,361	3,454	1,565	4,275	4,473

Source: Anuário Estatístico, Angola, 1970; Instituto Nacional de Estatística, Delegaçao de Angola, Luanda; *Estatística da Educaçao Ano Lectivo 1964–65,* Direcçao dos Serviços de Economia e Estatística Geral, Luanda.

1. Instituto Superior de Ciências Sociais e Política Ultramarina, *Moçambique,* op. cit., p. 544.
2. See: Allison Butler Herrick *et al., Area Handbook for Angola,* op. cit., p. 255.

Among the shorter films, the main increases were under the headings advertising, topical and recreative, as compared with an actual decrease under cultural. Portugal's interest in keeping control of the reporting of events in Portugal, the colonies, and elsewhere was reflected in the fact that Portugal produced hardly any long films at all, but produced 35 per cent of the short films on topical events that Angola imported.[1]

1. *Angola. Anuário Estatístico 1970*, Luanda.

Appendix 1

Newspapers and other periodicals in Angola [1]

Dailies

    A Província de Angola, Luanda
    Diàrio de Luanda, Luanda
    O Lobito, Lobito

Bi-weeklies

    O Apostolado, Luanda
    Jornal de Benguela, Benguela
    O Namibe, Moçâmedes

Weeklies

    Notícia, Luanda
    Actualidade Económica, Luanda
    Semana Ilustrada, Luanda
    Tribuno dos Musseques, Luanda
    A Palavra, Luanda
    O Campeão, Luanda
    Sul, Lobito
    Angola Norte, Malanje
    Jornal da Huíla, Sá da Bandeira
    Jornal do Congo, Carmona
    A Vóz do Bié, Silva Porto
    Ecos do Norte, Malanje

Fortnightlies

    Jornal Magazine, Luanda
    Revista de Angola, Luanda
    O Moxico, Luso

---

1. Written information by Centro de Informaçao e Turismo de Angola, Luanda, of 28 April 1973.

Jornal da Lunda, Henrique de Carvalho
Quanza Sul, Novo Redondo

Appearing every three weeks
    O Planalto, Nova Lisboa

Monthlies
    Prisma, Luanda
    Gazeta Agrícola, Luanda
    Revista 'O Turismo', Luanda

Periodicals appearing every six months (in order not to lose their periodical character)
    O Intransigente, Benguela
    A Huíla, Sá da Bandeira
    O Comércio, Luanda
    ABC—Diàrio de Angola, Luanda
    Angola Desportivo, Luanda
    Noite e Dia, Luanda

Appendix 2

Some data on radio stations in Angola

Station name	Power (kW)	Waveband	Frequencies (in kilocycles per second)	City
Rádio Clube de	1	Medium wave	1502	Benguela
Benguela	1	Short wave	3395[1]	
	1	Short wave	5045	
	0.2	Short wave	6150	
	0.1	FM	99.5	
Rádio Clube de	1	Medium wave	1349	Cabinda
Cabinda	1	Short wave	5035	
Rádio Diamang	1	Medium wave	1484	Dundo
Dundo	1	Short wave	4770	Portugália
	1	Short wave	9615	
Rádio Clube do	1	Medium wave	1115	Carmona
Uíge	1	Short wave	4860	
	0.1	FM	89840	
Rádio Clube do	1	Medium wave	1403	Lobito
Lobito	1	Short wave	4910	
	0.100	FM	94140	
A Voz de Luanda	0.25	Medium wave	1586	Luanda
Rádio Clube de	1	Medium wave	1232	Luanda
Angola	1	Short wave	4870	
	1	Short wave	7140	
	0.25	Short wave	9630	
	0.350	FM	89582	
Rádio Clube de	1	Medium wave	1214	Luso
Moxico	1	Short wave	5137	
Rádio Clube de	1	Medium wave	1331	Moçâmedes
Moçâmedes	1	Short wave	3215	

1. Belongs to the regional station of Cubal.

Station name	Power (kW)	Waveband	Frequencies (in kilocycles per second)	City
	0.75	Short wave	5015	
	3	FM	92.	
Rádio Clube de	1	Medium wave	1161	Malange
Malange	1	Short wave	4966	
	0.25	Short wave	3215	
Rádio Clube do	1 + 10	Medium wave	1160	Nova Lisboa
Humabo	1 + 10	Short wave	3345	
	1	Short wave	5060	
	1 + 10	Short wave	7160	
	1	Medium wave	1594	
	1	FM	97.	
Radio Clube da	1	Medium wave	1484	Novo
Cuanza-Sul	2	Short wave	4840	Redondo
Rádio Clube da	1	Medium wave	1313	Sá da
Huíla	1	Short wave	3970	Bandeira
	1	Short wave	5025	
	0.5	FM	93.5	
Rádio Comercial	1	Medium wave	1529	Sá da
de Angola	10	Short wave	4795; 7290	Bandeira
	0.1	FM	92162	
Emissora Nacio-	5	Short wave	4780	Serpa Pinto
nal de Menon-	5	Medium wave	1250	
gue				
Rádio Clube do	1	Medium wave	1385	Silva Porto
Bié	0.250	Short wave	3295	
	1	Short wave	4895	
	0.1	FM	88722	
Emissora Oficial	5	Medium wave	701	Luanda
de Angola	100	Medium wave	1088	
	10	Short wave	3375	
	10	Short wave	4820	
	10	Short wave	5960	
	10	Short wave	6175	
	10	Short wave	7245	
	100	Short wave	9535	
	100	Short wave	11875	
	0.1	FM	99.9	
	1	FM	95.538	
Voz de Angola	10 + 100	Medium wave	1367	Luanda
	100	Short wave	6115	
	10	Short wave	7265	
	100	Short wave	9660	
Rádio Eclésia	1	Medium wave	944	Luanda
	1	Short wave	4985; 7215	
	0.2	FM	97.5	

Station name	Power (kW)	Waveband	Frequencies (in kilocycles per second)	City
Voz de Cabinda (Emissora Regional)	5 5	Medium wave Short wave	1570 6025	Cabinda
Emissora Regional do Moxico	5 5	Medium wave Short wave	1421 5067	Luso
Emissora Regional de Saurimo	5 5	Medium wave Short wave	1241 4860	Henrique de Carvalho
Emissora Regional de Salazar	1	Medium wave	1160	Salazar
Emissora Regional do Zaire	10	Medium wave	1115	São Salvador

Source: Written information by Centro de Informação e Turismo de Angola, Luanda, 28 April 1973.